SEWING SCHOOL 2

Lessons in MACHINE SEWING

Amie Petronis Plumley & Andria Lisle

photography by Justin Fox Burks

Storey Publishing

The mission of Storey Publishing is to serve our customers by publishing practical information that encourages personal independence in harmony with the environment.

Edited by Deborah Balmuth and Beth Baumgartel
Art direction and book design by Jessica Armstrong

Photography by © Justin Fox Burks
Pattern diagrams by Missy Shepler

Indexed by Catherine Goddard

Storey Publishing
210 MASS MoCA Way
North Adams, MA 01247
www.storey.com

Printed in China by R.R. Donnelley
10 9 8 7 6 5

LIBRARY OF CONGRESS CATALOGING-IN-PUBLICATION DATA

Plumley, Amie Petronis.
  Sewing school 2 / by Amie Petronis Plumley and Andria Lisle ; photography by Justin Fox Burks.
    pages cm
  Includes index.
  ISBN 978-1-61212-049-2 (paper w/concealed wire-o and patterns : alk. paper
  ISBN 978-1-60342-896-5 (ebook)
  1. Sewing—Juvenile literature. I. Lisle, Andria. II. Burks, Justin Fox, illustrator.
  III. Title. IV. Title: Sewing school two.
  TT712.P59 2013
  646.4—dc23
                              2012042990

Dedicated to all the kids who have sewn with us,
both in person and through *Sewing School.*

ACKNOWLEDGMENTS

This book would not be without the cheerleading, love, and enthusiasm from so many.

To Grace-St. Luke's Episcopal School: GSL has become our home base for sewing with kids. Under the direction of headmaster Thor Kvande, the students, parents, teachers, and staff have embraced our mission and provided inspiration and encouragement. A special shout out to all the super sewers that attend our summer day camp and after school sewing club. You guys are the heart behind this book! Wendi Smith and the GSL Parent's Association for generously sharing their space with us. Martha Young and Emily Merrill for helping us whenever we needed it. Big hugs to Libby Shannon, Katie Donald, Cindy Sorrells, and Jill Beaumont for threading countless needles, offering advice, and helping to make our ideas a reality.

To our families: What would we do without you?! The constant talk of sewing, asking your opinion about things you know nothing about, and covering for us when we were working on deadlines. Kisses to Eric, Phoebe, and Frankie Plumley; Betty, Maclin, Jeff, and Mary Ann Lisle, as well as Levon Williams and the staff at the Memphis Brooks Museum of Art, Amy Lawrence, Graham, III, and Bianca Burks.

To everyone at Storey Publishing: We are so lucky to be working with a publisher that truly understands our message. Deborah, Pam, Beth, Alee, Jess, Jessica, and Mars — you guys rock!

To helpful friends: Cynthia Mann at Birch Fabrics for generously supplying us with fabric for the Patchwork Scarf — we couldn't imagine using anything else! Doug Halijan for his expert advice and Kevin Barré, for his fabulous author photos. Mary Alllison Cates and Susan Schwartz at Sew Memphis for including us in their fabric store dreams!

To the readers of *Sewing School* and our blog: You validate what we are doing, and we love sharing ideas and seeing your wonderful creations.

CONTENTS

A Note to You from the Authors

Hello! We're delighted to discover that so many kids love sewing as much as we do. When we were young like you, we couldn't wait to learn how to sew and make things all by ourselves.

When Amie was just a little girl, she would watch over her mother's shoulder as her mom made all kinds of things on the sewing machine. When she got a little bit older, her mom taught her how to use a sewing machine on her own. Soon, Amie was making her own clothes and fun things for her room! She didn't get her very own sewing machine until after she graduated from college, but now Amie has two machines set up side by side; one for her to use, and one for her daughter, Phoebe.

Andria also grew up watching her mama sew. One Christmas, when she was about six years old, Andria found a funny little sewing machine under the tree. It was a toy, and instead of a needle and thread, it had a sticky glue cartridge that would glue fabrics together. It was a mess, but Andria was finally making things on her own, like blankets for her stuffed animals and clothes for them to wear. Soon after, she began to use her mom's sewing machine, although she had to slow down and be more careful because she was working with a real needle and operating an electric machine.

Now that we're finally adults, we sew all the time. Amie makes all kinds of clothes for her entire family. She also teaches kindergarten and runs an after-school sewing club for her students. Andria likes to decorate her house with all the things she's sewn. She works at an art museum, and loves to look at the beautiful quilts and textiles that are part of the museum's permanent collection.

In our free time, we like to teach children how to sew. Every summer, we hold a Sewing School day camp at Amie's school. During one session, we teach hand sewing. The idea for our first book, *Sewing School: 21 Sewing Projects Kids Will Love to Make*, was born in our first Sewing School camp. Our summer camp sessions were so popular that we added a second class. In the second class our students, all between the ages of 7 and 13, used sewing machines to test-sew the projects in this book.

Like our campers, after you've practiced hand sewing for a while, you will be ready to move on to a sewing machine. If you've ever looked at other sewing books or sewing patterns, you might think that sewing with a machine, using patterns, and following detailed directions can be really tricky and bewildering, but it's really not. Don't worry, even we get confused sometimes! Our hopes are that after sewing some of the basic projects in this book, you'll be ready for more complex projects, and that soon you'll be making whatever you want.

Writing this book was very important to both of us because we want kids everywhere to be able to learn how to use a sewing machine. Now, with this book by your side, you don't have to live near us to learn how to sew. You can do it whenever and wherever you want.

We can't wait for you to make all kinds of stuff on your sewing machine. Let's get started!

Happy Sewing!
Amie & Andria

Amie Petronis Plumley & Andria Lisle

An Introduction for Adults

Sewing School 2 inspires children and teaches them how to sew on a sewing machine. It features step-by-step directions, simple language, and child-created examples of contemporary projects, all made on a sewing machine.

Children are fascinated by the sewing machine. And once they learn how to safely operate one, they can easily create any of the projects in this book with minimal supervision or help. These projects build on prior knowledge, or "step-up projects." Each project includes a reference for adult support, called "A Note for Grown-Ups," which will provide detailed guidance on steps that might require adult assistance. The step-by-step directions are written at a second-grade comprehension level, with projects designed for sewers ages seven and older.

Please don't purchase a toy sewing machine and expect your child to be able to use it to make the projects in this book. Toy machines are usually plastic and poorly made, which will only frustrate young sewers. If you're looking for a kid-friendly sewing machine, we like the sturdy and practical Janome Sew Mini Sewing Machine. Children can also use adult sewing machines. If you're buying a used machine, you might want to take it to a repair shop for routine maintenance before your child

begins to use it, as there is nothing more frustrating than using a sewing machine that doesn't properly work!

If your sewer is very young or particularly inexperienced, start by moving the sewing machine pedal to a tabletop and allowing the child to press it with one hand to make the needle go. Show your child how to raise and lower the presser foot, and gently guide the fabric while you remain in control. After a few sessions, your child should be able to handle rudimentary sewing skills on his or her own.

Other than a sewing machine, this craft requires only a few inexpensive tools. You'll mainly need fabric, thread, and a pair of scissors, plus an assortment of trims and notions, depending on the project. (For our tried-and-true recommendations, refer to the Resource Guide in the back of this book.)

Be sure to discuss safety with your sewer. Stress the fact that a sewing machine is not a toy. Emphasize the importance of asking for adult help when needed, particularly when it comes to replacing a sewing machine needle or using an iron. Help find an out-of-the way work space to set up the sewing machine. Letting a child have unsupervised access to a sewing machine might feel a little bit perilous.

Only you can decide how much freedom your young sewer deserves. Generally speaking, if a child is mature enough to treat a sewing machine with respect, there is no reason for you to hover.

As children learn to sew, they improve their fine motor skills and learn how to focus and follow directions. Once they start sewing, some children will repeatedly ask mid-project, "What's next?" Refer your sewer back to the book, which has detailed written and photographed steps. Try to step back and let them discover new skills, figure out how to

fix mistakes, and learn the "whys" of sewing as they become more self-sufficient. Young sewers learn vital lessons that will help them in other facets of life, such as how to follow directions, not to skip important steps, and, with many of the projects in this book, how to complete a project that might take more than one day. They will gain self-esteem as they create something complex out of simple materials, and their imaginations will flourish.

When it comes to the projects in this book, encourage your kids to "Make It Yours" by devising their own design details and changing shapes and details as they wish. By learning that there are many different ways to complete a project, they will gain confidence in their abilities and take their inventiveness to new levels. We purposely kept our examples of each project simple, so that young sewers can elaborate on their own.

Regardless of your own sewing skills, we hope that you have fun crafting with your child. Don't get hung up on straight seams or even hems, especially in the beginning. One of our rules for young sewers and their helpers is "Nothing has to be perfect." Imperfections give each project an individual flair and a uniqueness that cannot be found in any mass-produced merchandise. Sharing the gift of sewing is one of the greatest, most creative things you can do for your child. It is a skill that will last a lifetime and might even be passed down to future generations, too.

Welcome to Sewing School 2!

Sewing with a machine looks hard. Sewing with a machine seems magical and a little bit dangerous, too. If you follow the instructions in this book, you can learn how to safely and successfully use a sewing machine.

And once you know how to sew, you can make whatever you want using fabric, thread, and your sewing machine. All of the projects in this book were kid-tested by sewers between the ages 7 and 13.

You might already be familiar with a sewing machine. Maybe your grandmother has one that she uses to make clothes. Maybe your mom or dad has a sewing machine that is stored on a closet shelf or sits on its own table in your family's craft room. Maybe they've let you operate the foot pedal while they guide the fabric under the needle. Or maybe no one else in your family has ever sewed at all. Whether you've inherited a sewing machine, just bought one, or are planning to start sewing soon, this book will help you become a careful, independent sewer. Use the step-by-step pictures and directions included with each project to learn how to safely use a sewing machine without any help from grown-ups.

Before you jump in and start a big sewing project, please read through this entire chapter. It will teach you so much that will make sewing any project easier. It includes twelve lessons that teach the basics of machine sewing, like how to identify the parts of a sewing machine, how to thread a machine and make a bobbin, and how to sew basic machine stitches. You can also refer back to these specific lessons as you make all the projects in this book.

How to Use This Book

Sewing School 2 is filled with step-by-step pictures and directions that make it easy to learn how to sew. We've added guides to make sure that everything goes smoothly so you'll have lots of fun. Here is a list of the kinds of guides you'll find with each project.

Ratings

Each project is rated with one, two, or three stars so you will know how easy it is to make. If you are new to using a sewing machine, you can start with one-star projects and work your way up to the three-star projects.

⭐ **One star** means it is an easy project. It is perfect for new sewers. You will use very basic skills to sew just a few pieces of fabric together. You can make a one-star project in about an hour.

⭐⭐ **Two stars** means it is a skill-building project. These projects teach new skills, such as putting in a zipper and working with bigger pieces of fabric. You might want to spend all afternoon or even a few days to finish a two-star project.

⭐⭐⭐ **Three stars** means it is a harder project. These projects feature steps that are meant to challenge you, such as quilting, or adding a layer of batting. Three-star projects have more steps than the other projects and might take days or even a week to sew.

"I learned how to use a sewing machine this year, and it was a little easier than I thought!"
— CATE, 10

What You Need

This is a list of the fabric and supplies you need to make the project.

Let's Review

This is a short list of the skills you'll need to know to sew the project. If you are unsure about a skill, you can go back and review it before you begin the project.

Make It Yours

All of the projects in this book are very basic. It is up to you to make them special. Here, you'll find a few ideas for putting your own stamp on a project.

A Note for Grown-Ups

This is a message for your parent or another adult who might be helping you sew the project.

Skill Check

With some projects, you'll have the opportunity to learn a new skill. The skill check teaches you all the steps you'll need to know.

11

How to Choose a Sewing Machine

*If you don't already have a sewing machine you can use, you'll need to find one.
Maybe someone in your family or a friend has a machine you can borrow.
If you have to buy a machine, used machines are easy to find.*

There are also new machines for sale at very affordable prices. Ask a grown-up to help you find one that fits your budget and is suitable for your needs. Look for a real (not toy) sewing machine that is simple and easy to operate. While there are a lot of cute toy sewing machines available, you will need a real machine to successfully complete the projects in this book. If you're a first-time machine sewer, and you're looking for a small, affordable sewing machine, check out the Janome Sew Mini. We recommend this machine because it is portable and very easy for a kid to use and understand.

Since cabinetmaker Thomas Saint invented the sewing machine in England during the Industrial Revolution, thousands of brands and models have come on the market. Just make sure that your sewing machine has a drop-in bobbin mechanism (not a side-loading bobbin) because it is easier for beginning sewers to operate.

Whether you buy a new or used machine, make sure the operating manual is with it. Avoid purchasing a sewing machine without a manual. If you can't find a manual, or just for extra help, you can ask a grown-up to search Google or YouTube for helpful videos that show you how to perform important tasks like loading the bobbin or threading your machine.

WHAT TO LOOK FOR IN A SEWING MACHINE

* *Real machine (not toy)*
* *Fits your space and budget*
* *Drop-in bobbin*
* *Manual available*

"When you start out, you might want to look for a smaller machine, because you can always advance to a bigger machine once you get better at sewing."

– LAUREN, 11

Anatomy of a Sewing Machine

All sewing machines are a bit different, but they all have the same important parts. Each part plays an important role. Here is an example of a basic sewing machine. You might also need to refer to your manual to locate some of the parts on your particular machine.

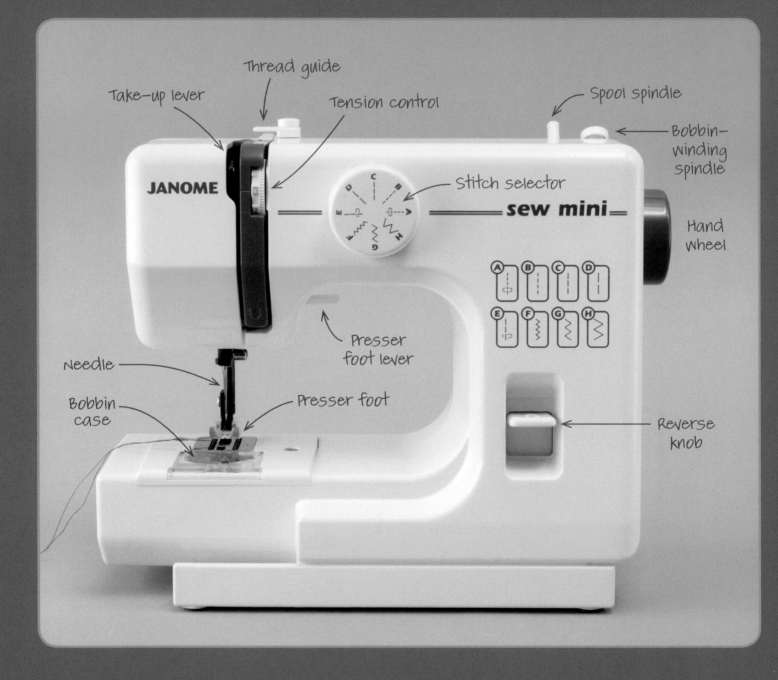

Thread guide

Take-up lever

Tension control

Spool spindle

Bobbin-winding spindle

JANOME

Stitch selector

sew mini

Hand wheel

Presser foot lever

Needle

Bobbin case

Presser foot

Reverse knob

FEED DOGS – These rough-feeling teeth are located below the presser foot, on the needle plate of your sewing machine. Feed dogs will gently pull the fabric through the machine.

FOOT PEDAL – A sewing machine foot pedal works just like the accelerator of a car. Push down to go fast, and ease up to slow down. Some models of sewing machines also have a speed control. Always take your foot off the pedal and put it flat on the floor before you make adjustments on your sewing machine, such as raising or lowering the needle.

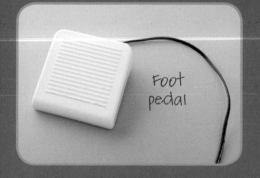
Foot pedal

HAND WHEEL – Use the hand wheel to slowly operate your sewing machine needle. Turn the wheel toward you to raise or lower the needle.

NEEDLE PLATE – Located under the sewing machine's presser foot and over the bobbin casing, the needle plate surrounds the point of your needle and the feed dogs. Look closely at the needle

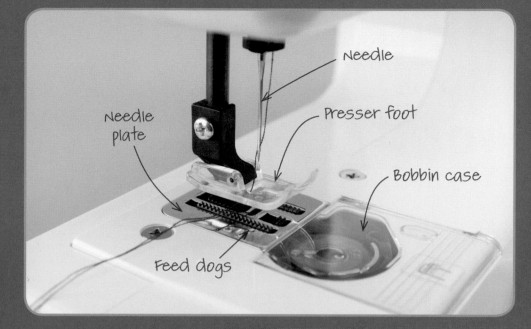
Needle plate
Needle
Presser foot
Bobbin case
Feed dogs

plate on most machines, and you'll see a seam guide that will help you keep your seam allowances at the right width. Most needle plates are removable to replace a drop-in bobbin or to clean lint and loose threads from underneath.

PRESSER FOOT – This sewing machine part works like an extra pair of fingers that help guide the fabric as it moves under the needle. You can raise and lower the presser foot using a lever on the back of your machine. Many sewing machines come with extra presser foots that can be switched according to the task at hand, like making buttonholes or sewing in a zipper. We recommend that beginning sewers stick with an all-purpose presser foot.

STITCH SELECTOR – This control knob on your sewing machine will determine what kind of stitch you might make. On basic sewing machines, you can choose between straight or zigzag stitches. Fancier machines have many more varieties of stitches.

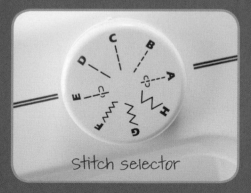
Stitch selector

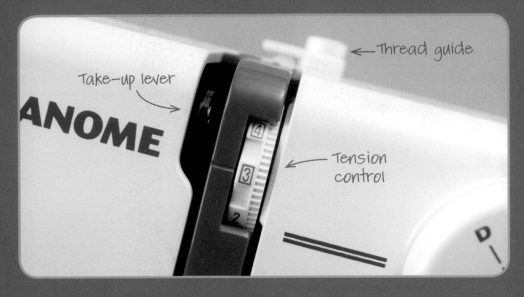

Take-up lever

Thread guide

Tension control

More Sewing Terms You Need to Know

BOBBIN – A sewing machine bobbin is a very small spool of thread that fits inside your sewing machine in a space called the bobbin casing. As you press the foot pedal and the needle flies in and out of the top side of your fabric, the bobbin thread sews the bottom side. Every brand and model of sewing machine uses its own style and size of bobbin, so be sure you've got the correct bobbin for your machine. Keep a supply of extra bobbins in your sewing kit. You will wind thread onto the bobbins yourself, following directions on page 27.

TAKE-UP LEVER – This arm is a very important part of threading the sewing machine. It moves up and down as the needle moves up and down in and out of your fabric. Use the hand wheel to move the take-up lever to its highest position whenever you're about to thread it. If your thread is clumping and making a mess when you sew, you might have forgotten to guide the thread through the take-up lever.

TENSION CONTROL – This knob controls the delicate relationship between your sewing thread and your bobbin thread. You should not have to adjust it often. If necessary, refer to your sewing machine manual to make sure that you maintain the perfect tension level — you don't want one thread looser or tighter than the other one. Be very careful when adjusting the tension control. If it gets too unbalanced, you might have to take your sewing machine to a repair shop to get it rebalanced.

THREAD GUIDES – These are little locks, levers, and loops that you must direct the thread through on its way from the spool to your machine's needle. Many sewing machines use arrows or numbered or lettered labels to remind you how to guide the thread. Or, refer to your sewing machine manual for exact details.

BODKIN – This is a tool that will help you pull elastic or string through a casing. If you don't have a bodkin, you can use a large safety pin instead.

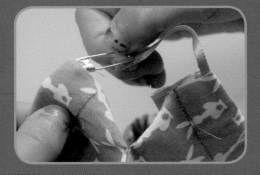

PINKING SHEARS – These special sewing scissors have sawtooth blades, which leave a zigzag edge instead of a straight edge. If you don't want to hem a finished project, try using pinking shears instead of regular scissors to cut the edge of the fabric. Pinking shears help reduce the amount of fraying. They can also be used for decoration. Experiment by using pinking shears to cut the open edge of a pocket before you sew it onto your project.

REINFORCE STITCH – This is a variation on the reverse stitch. You will use the reinforce stitch when you need your stitches to be extra-strong, such as when you attach the handles on projects like the eHold or the Portable Tree Stump or the elastic band on the Art-to-Go-Go.

REVERSE STITCH – Reversing is what knots your thread, so your stitches can't come undone later on. It's important to reverse stitch when you start sewing a stitch, and to reverse again at the end to "lock" it. Your manual will tell you how to locate the reverse knob or button on your sewing machine.

STAY STITCH – A stay stitch is a quick and simple straight stitch that will help keep cotton fabric from fraying too much. You will sew a stay stitch in place of a hem when you make the Snack Time Bag, and on other projects that have pockets.

STOP & START SEWING MARKS – The marks that you make on your fabric when you are going to leave a space to turn your project good side out or stuff it. You will make these marks yourself with chalk. They should be as far apart as the length of your pointer finger.

STRAIGHT STITCH – This is the most basic stitch you can sew using a machine. Just as it sounds, it looks like a straight line. It's also the stitch you'll use most often. The straight stitch makes perfect seams when you're sewing together two pieces of fabric. It can also be used for hemming, topstitching, or decorating almost-finished projects.

In Your Sewing Kit

If you already know how to hand sew, you probably have a sewing kit of your own. Your machine sewing kit will look a lot like a grown-up's sewing kit, with inexpensive tools that you can use over and over again. Be sure to keep all your sewing tools in one place. We recommend using a medium-size box or bag for your very own sewing kit.

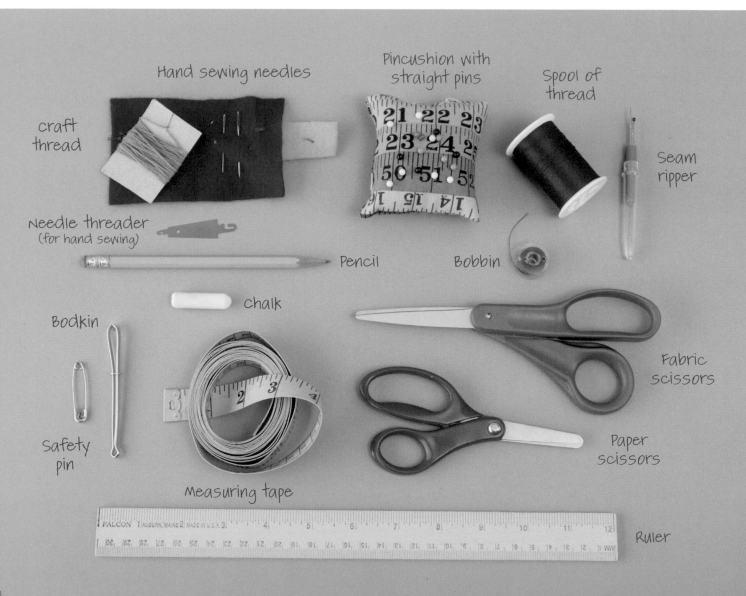

Hand sewing needles

Pincushion with straight pins

Spool of thread

craft thread

Seam ripper

Needle threader (for hand sewing)

Pencil

Bobbin

chalk

Bodkin

Fabric scissors

Safety pin

Paper scissors

Measuring tape

Ruler

Here is a list of the tools and notions you need for your sewing kit. You can find more information about these tools in the Resource Guide in the back of this book.

Sewing Machine Bobbins

Bobbins that are the right size for your sewing machine are key to quick and easy sewing. Wind (page 27) one or two with thread so you can just slip in a new bobbin when the bobbin you are using runs out of thread. Keep two or three bobbins empty so you can wind them with specific colors to match or contrast your fabric.

Needles

* **Sewing machine needles.** Keep a supply of different size needles on hand and use a new needle after about eight hours of sewing on your machine. For normal sewing, we like to use size 14 needles. If you have heavier fabrics like fleece or denim, you might need a larger needle (size 16 or 18). Smaller needles (size 8 or 10) are suitable for lightweight fabrics.

* **Hand sewing needles.** You'll use these to finish stuffed projects or add trimmings. You can use a Chenille Size 22 Sharp Point Needle and craft thread, especially when you want to show off your hand sewing stitches. Or, when you want to hide your stitches, you might prefer to use a regular sewing needle and the same thread you use on your sewing machine.

Thread

* **Machine sewing thread.** Start with a spool of white thread and then add spools of other colors as you need them. It's easy to get overwhelmed when you look at all the types of thread available at the fabric store, but all-purpose sewing thread works great for most projects.

* **Hand sewing thread.** You might want some craft thread or thicker thread so the stitches show and become part of the design.

Scissors

Scissors are a very important part of your sewing kit. You will use them to cut fabric and thread. We recommend the Fiskars Junior scissors. Never cut paper (including sewing patterns) with your sewing scissors because paper will make them dull. Keep another pair of scissors in your sewing kit for cutting out paper patterns. We like to call these scissors "everything else scissors," because you will use them to cut everything *but* fabric. You might also want to have a pair of pinking shears in your sewing kit. They are special sewing scissors that have sawtooth blades instead of a straight edge.

Chalk and Pencil

Use chalk or a pencil to trace patterns and measurements on fabric. Chalk works great when you need to make a temporary mark on your fabric, because you can rub it off afterward. There are also fabric-marking pencils that you can use to trace patterns and rub off afterward, too.

CRAFT THREAD

TIP: Tie a piece of ribbon on the handle of your fabric scissors so you remember to only use them on fabric. Or, use a marker to label the scissors handle.

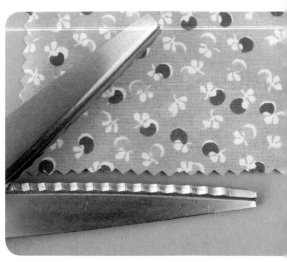

Pinking shears give your project a zigzag edge.

"My manual helps me when I'm stuck with things."
— CATE, 10

Ruler or Measuring Tape

A ruler or measuring tape will help you measure exactly where you need to cut and sew. A ruler works best when you're working on a table or on the floor. Use the measuring tape when you need to measure items that are not flat, such as people or toys.

Bodkin or Large Safety Pin

Either of these will be useful when you are pulling elastic or a drawstring through a casing.

Pincushion and Straight Pins

You'll need straight pins (with large, round heads) to pin a pattern to your fabric or to hold two pieces of fabric together while you are sewing. Pins are sharp! Be sure to use a pincushion so you always know where your pins are! To find out how to pin, see page 47.

Seam Ripper

This small, sharp metal tool will help you undo your sewing machine mistakes. Keep it near your sewing machine. Learn how to correctly use a seam ripper on page 153.

Sewing Machine Manual

Many different manufacturers make sewing machines, and while they all basically work the same way, each machine is a little bit different. You will often need to be able to refer to the manual, or guide, for your particular machine. If you can't find the manual for your sewing machine, you might be able to locate a copy online. Or, ask a friend who sews to help write down basic instructions for your machine.

Sewing Machine School Rules

1. Set up your sewing machine in a safe place.

This is very important. You need to find a table or desk with an electrical outlet nearby where you can safely use your machine. If possible, stay out of the way of family traffic. Don't sew at the kitchen table while the grown-ups are trying to cook dinner. Try to keep your work space clean and free of other clutter so you can spread out your sewing project. Make sure you have a lamp nearby or a bright overhead light because it's easy to get frustrated if you can't see exactly what you're doing. Sit in a chair that's the right height so you can easily reach the foot pedal from your seat.

2. Your sewing machine is not a toy!

There is a lot of responsibility that comes with using a real sewing machine. We know it's tempting to stomp on that foot pedal and watch your needle and thread race from one end of the fabric to the other, but that's not safe or smart. You can break your machine doing this, or even worse, hurt yourself or someone else. Do you know what it feels like to accidentally prick your finger with a hand sewing needle? Sewing machine needles are even sharper, and they make quick, tiny stitches that can really hurt your fingers. But, as long as you use your sewing machine correctly, you will be fine. Once you've got your rhythm, it's easy to let your mind wander as you zip from one end of the fabric to the other. Pay attention! You can easily bend or break your sewing machine needle. Don't ever run over a pin, a zipper pull, or anything else that's metal. If you're using pins, pause when the presser foot comes close to the place you've pinned. Take your foot off the pedal. Remove the pin and put it in your pincushion, then resume sewing.

Stop and pull out pins before your needle runs over them.

3. Iron safely.

Never, ever iron without adult supervision. Irons are very hot, and it's too easy to accidentally burn yourself. You must always use an ironing board. Never use an iron on the floor or a bed. Make sure the electrical cord isn't stretched where you or someone else could trip over it and knock over the iron. Don't ever leave the iron in the "down" position on your fabric. Unplug the iron immediately after using it and let it cool for at least an hour before you put it away.

4. Nothing has to be perfect.

The projects that you sew might not look like something you bought in a store, but that's okay, because you made it yourself. Sewing machine mistakes aren't quite as easy to undo as hand sewing mistakes, but at the end of this book, we'll give you some advice for undoing stitches and fixing some problems (page 153).

5. Take your time.

When you first use a sewing machine, you'll feel like you're sewing fast, fast, fast, because the machine is doing all the work. However, sewing is not a race. Relax, and slow down, because none of these projects have to be completed in a single day. When you want to take a break, pick out a good stopping point, put your project in a plastic bag that zips closed, and turn off your machine.

"If you iron the good sides down first it looks nicer and is easier to sew."
— PHOEBE, 7

TIP: If you don't have permission to use an iron, you can always use your fingers to smooth down the fabric before you start to sew.

Finding Out about Fabric

Choosing the right fabric for your sewing project is very important. When you pick a project in this book to make, read through the directions to see if you need to use a particular kind of fabric before you start sewing. If not, you can pick any kind of fabric you like.

With a grown-up's permission, you can also shop for fabrics right inside your own house. Ask if you can have old sheets and pillowcases or other large pieces of material for your fabric stash. Maybe you've outgrown clothes that you can cut up to make something new. Just be sure to ask first!

Here is a little bit about the fabrics that you will use to make the projects in this book.

Cotton

Cotton fabric is easy to cut and sew, but it frays, or fringes, when you cut it. Examine a new piece of cotton fabric that you've purchased at a fabric store, and you'll notice that one edge of the fabric is finished with a special weave that won't fray. This edge of the fabric is called the selvage. Look closely and you might see the name of the company or the fabric design printed along the selvage. Usually this edge of fabric is trimmed off and discarded when you cut out your patterns.

When you're choosing cotton fabric, there are millions of colors and patterns that you can pick from. Find a store near you that sells printed fabric or refer to the Resource Guide in the back of this book to find a place. You can even design your own using muslin (thin, oatmeal-colored cotton fabric) and fabric markers!

At fabric stores, cotton fabric is stored on big bolts. Most cotton fabrics are sold by the yard (3 feet of material at a time). You'll need about ½ yard of fabric to make most of the projects in this book.

Good side. Cotton fabric has two sides, a front and a back. Pay attention to the front, or good side, of the fabric when you're cutting and sewing. The good side of the fabric is the one where you can see the print really well. On the other side, the print looks faded. You want to make certain that the good side of the cotton ends up on the outside of your project. This can get a little bit tricky when you're sewing on a machine, because most often, you'll sew with the good sides together and then turn the project good side out when you're finished.

Cotton frays when cut

luna for birch fabrics

Selvage

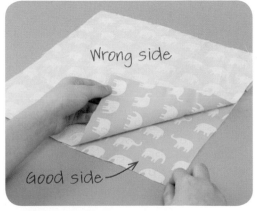

Wrong side

Good side

"One-way fabric is when the animals or whatever the pattern is faces one direction. You'll know if you fold it, because then the pattern will be upside down."

— PHOEBE, 7

ALL-OVER PRINT

ONE-WAY PRINT

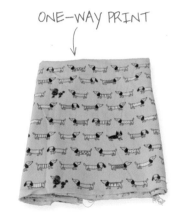

FELT

FLANNEL

FLEECE

All-over print. Before you start cutting and sewing, keep in mind the pattern, or print, on your cotton fabric. Some fabrics have an all-over pattern, like this zoo fabric, and others have a print that goes in one direction. The animals on the zoo fabric are printed every which way, so there's no "top" or "bottom."

One-way print. Fabrics that have a direction are a bit harder to work with because you need all the fabric pieces to go in one direction. Take a close look at the dog fabric above. See how all of the dogs have heads and tails that point upward? Those heads and tails also need to point upward when your project is finished. Keep this in mind when you're laying out your pattern pieces and cutting out the fabric for your project. Or, if you're not careful, the print might wind up upside down.

If you buy new cotton fabric, wash it before you use it, because cotton will shrink a little bit when it gets wet. Afterward, you might need to iron it to get out the wrinkles. If so, ask a grown-up for help.

Felt

Felt is a great fabric to sew because it doesn't fray, so you don't have to hem it. Felt especially comes in handy when you want to make a quick pocket on a project like the Secret Message Pillow, or when you're working with small pieces of fabric, such as the Cookie Coin Saver. Felt is thick and colorful and bright on both sides.

Flannel

There's a reason why in the olden days pajamas and long johns were made out of flannel. It's because this fabric, traditionally made from cotton or wool, is as soft and as warm as fleece, but much thinner and easier to sew. Flannel, like cotton, has a good side, so you'll have to remember that when you are cutting and sewing it.

Fleece

Fleece is very similar to felt, but it is softer and doesn't feel as scratchy against your skin. It's also like flannel, but it's a much thicker fabric.

> **TIP:** Sewing through two or more layers of fleece can be difficult because the fabric is very thick. If you are using a Janome Sew Mini sewing machine, the fleece might bunch up.

Patterns

Before using the patterns that come with this book, you will have to cut them out. Cut the paper on the solid lines and remember to use your "everything else" scissors, not your sewing scissors! Once your patterns are cut out, you can store them in the back of this book. You can also copy them or trace them to make new patterns.

Once you've picked a project to make, find all of the pattern pieces. Read how many times you will have to trace the pattern and then cut out the fabric, and keep this in mind when choosing which fabric you want to use. If you're using cotton fabric, don't forget to pay attention to the pattern, or print. If it's an all-over print, you can lay out the pattern pieces in any direction. If it's a one-way print (page 25), you need to think through all the steps of the project before you lay out and cut out your patterns.

Before you start laying out your fabric, read the instructions because some of the projects in this book require you to fold the fabric in half before cutting it.

For a single layer of fabric, smooth out your fabric on a flat surface (the kitchen table or a wood floor works great). Place the pattern on top of the fabric near one edge. Use your chalk or a pencil to trace around the pattern. If you are having trouble keeping the pattern in place, it helps to pin the pattern to the fabric first. Or you can ask a friend to help hold down the pattern. If you don't have a helper,

use a heavy can to hold your pattern and fabric in place.

For a double layer of fabric, fold the fabric so the selvage, or finished edges, match and carefully follow the instructions included with the project. All of the patterns in this book were designed with a seam allowance of ¼ inch (see page 33).

If you're designing your own creation and you need to make a pattern, try drawing on cardboard, card stock, or a brown paper bag that is too thick to tear. Don't forget to include a seam allowance on your original patterns. Otherwise, the patterns will be too small.

"Don't just pay attention to the fabric. Pay attention to the directions on the sewing pattern, too!"
— MARY CLAIRE, 8

Ready, Set, Thread

Two really important steps in machine sewing are making a bobbin and correctly threading your sewing machine. While it's tempting to just ask a helpful grown-up to do these tasks for you, you'll become a better sewer if you learn how to do them yourself. Plus, you won't have to wait around for an adult to have the time to help.

How to Make a Bobbin

A sewing machine bobbin is a very small spool of thread that fits inside your sewing machine. As you press the foot pedal and the needle flies in and out of the top of your fabric, the bobbin thread sews the bottom side of the fabric. Every brand and model of sewing machine uses its own style and size of bobbin, so be sure you've got the correct bobbin for your machine. You will want to use the same thread that you're using on the top of your machine to make your bobbin.

Refer to the manual that goes with your sewing machine because every machine works differently. Here is how to make a bobbin on this machine; the process is similar for most machines.

> **TIP:** On some machines, you need to stop the needle from going up and down while you make the bobbin. Check your manual to find out how to stop the needle.

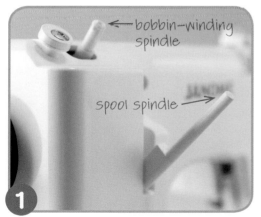

1 Place your thread onto the machine's spool spindle and then run the end of thread over and through the bobbin-winding tension disk on your machine.

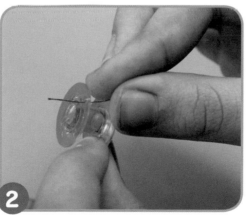

2 Poke the end of the thread through the tiny hole in the top of the empty bobbin from the inside out. Make sure you have a tail of thread that is about 5 inches long sticking out of the top.

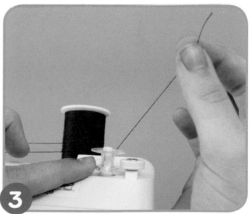

3 Push the bobbin onto the bobbin-winding spindle until it is all the way down on the post. Put it on so that the tail of the thread coming through the bobbin hole sticks up like a little flag. Push the bobbin spindle to the right.

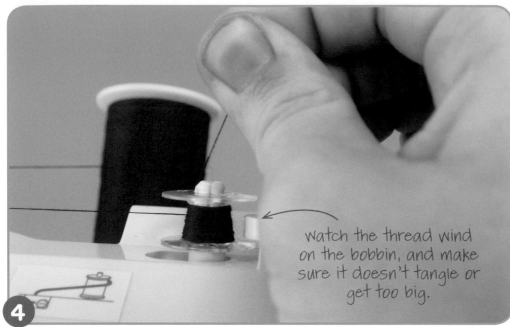

Watch the thread wind on the bobbin, and make sure it doesn't tangle or get too big.

4 Reach up and hold the little flag of thread. Make sure your fingers are out of the way of any moving machine parts, and s-l-o-w-l-y press the foot pedal. If everything is correct, the bobbin spindle will turn.

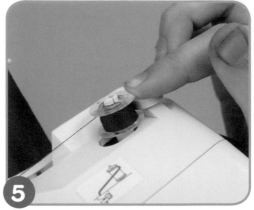

5 Continue to wind the thread slowly, so it doesn't stretch and break and it isn't too loose or too tight. Let the thread wrap around the bobbin until it nearly fills the bobbin spool. Some machines will tell you when to stop winding, but it's important to pay attention. Otherwise, your bobbin will cause problems later on!

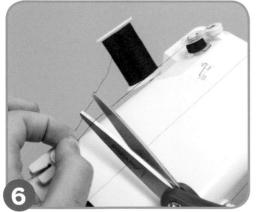

6 Once your bobbin is wound, cut the thread between the big spool and the bobbin. Then cut the little flag as close to the bobbin as possible, so it can't tangle up your thread once it is loaded into your machine.

7 Load the bobbin into the machine according to the directions in your sewing machine manual.

TIP: Never try to add thread to a bobbin that already has some thread on it. Either remove the thread or find an empty bobbin.

How to Thread Your Machine

Again, refer to your sewing machine manual because every machine is a little bit different. Threading is like a roller coaster ride — you go down, up, and down again before finally threading the needle.

1 Put your thread on the spool pin. Most machines have a numbered guide or little arrows printed right on the machine. Guide your thread from right to left through the eyelet on top of the machine. Now you're going to go down all the way to the tension area on the left side of the machine. Guide the thread around the tension dial.

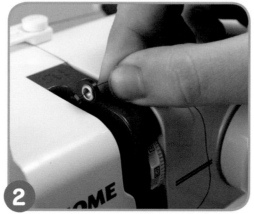

2 You'll go back down to the take-up lever, the metal arm that rises up and down as you sew. Slowly turn the hand wheel toward you to move the arm to its highest position so you can push your thread through the take-up lever.

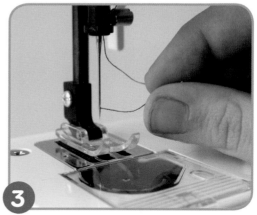

3 Follow your machine's instructions to guide the thread down to the needle. If your sewing machine has a light, turn it on, because that will help you see the tiny hole, or eye, in the needle. Thread the needle from front to back.

TIP: If your thread is a little bit frayed from guiding it through your machine, use scissors to trim the end.

How to Get Your Bobbin Thread

Now it's time to get the bobbin thread. Once again, the manual will be a big help here. Now you understand why it's so important to have a manual and keep it near your workstation!

1 If you haven't already installed your bobbin in the machine, do so now.

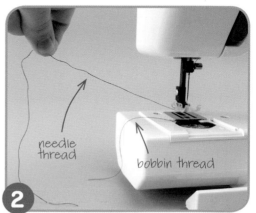

needle thread

bobbin thread

2 Make sure a length of bobbin thread is extending beyond the actual bobbin. Hold the needle thread with your left hand.

3

Continue to hold the needle thread in your left hand. Use your right hand to slowly turn the hand wheel toward you.

you caught the bobbin thread!

4

Watch as the needle drops down beneath the needle plate and comes back up. It should grab the bobbin thread and bring it up so you can see it. The bobbin thread will be looped up by the needle.

5

Using a straight pin, find the loop and pull it away from the needle to bring the end of the bobbin thread up through the needle plate.

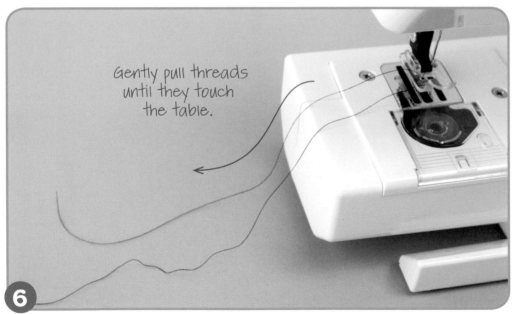

Gently pull threads until they touch the table.

6

Gently grab the ends of both threads, and give them a very slight tug so that you have about 5 inches of both threads trailing away from the left side of the needle plate. Replace the bobbin cover.

THE TABLE RULE

Every time you finish sewing, lift the needle and the presser foot and gently pull the fabric off the sewing machine. Now, as gently as you can, pull the threads down to the tabletop. Clip them close to the fabric instead of close to the machine. Make sure you have enough extra thread to reach your table. *Now you're ready to sew the next time!*

Get Your Machine Stitches On

Your sewing machine is threaded with its spool of thread and its bobbin, and you're ready to go.

Here are the three kinds of stitches you will use to sew the projects in this book. Of course, there are many other stitches, but you only need to know how to make these three. Use the stitch selection dial or button on your machine to set your machine to the stitch you want to use before you start sewing.

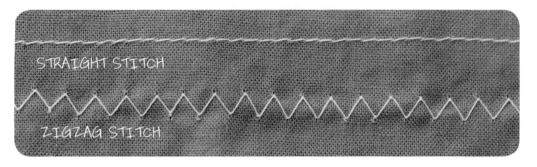

STRAIGHT STITCH

ZIGZAG STITCH

The Straight Stitch

This is the most basic stitch you can sew using a machine. It's also the one you'll use most often. Just as it sounds, it looks like a straight line. The straight stitch makes perfect seams when you're sewing together two pieces of fabric. It can also be used for topstitching, or decorating almost-finished projects. And once you get a few projects under your belt, you'll realize that the straight stitch is useful to hem the edges of fabric.

The Zigzag Stitch

For first-time sewing machine users, the zigzag stitch is a little bit like a party. Compared to the straight stitch, it's like eating Cheetos for breakfast instead of a bowl of cereal. Because the thread zigs and zags, this is a wider stitch than a straight stitch, so when you use it, make sure you have plenty of seam allowance. You can use the zigzag stitch to decorate your projects, but keep in mind that you'll need to do this in the beginning, because you won't be able to zigzag once your fabric is sewn together or stuffed. The zigzag stitch also makes a great hem when you're sewing cotton fabric.

The Reverse Stitch

Knowing how to reverse stitch is very important. Reversing is what knots your thread, so your stitches don't come undone later on. It's important to reverse stitch when you start sewing a seam and to reverse again at the end to "lock" it. Refer to your sewing machine manual to locate the reverse knob or button on your sewing machine. Hint: it's usually marked with a circular arrow. Many projects in this book require a reinforce stitch (page 34), which is the same as a reverse stitch.

If you have a newer sewing machine, you probably have the ability to choose from a selection of cool stitches. Experiment on a piece of scrap fabric by practicing all the stitches your machine can make. You might find some beautiful stitches that you can use to draw a picture or design on your fabric. However, keep in mind that when it comes to sewing the projects in this book, it will be best to use the stitches recommended in the instructions. You can also experiment with different colors of thread. Most sewers use white thread or a color that matches the fabric so that it blends in. Sometimes it's more fun to choose a contrasting color of thread that will show off your stitches.

You can practice making all these stitches by creating the Stitching Sampler on page 42.

It's Time to Sew

You have already found out about different kinds of fabric, you know about patterns, and you've learned about the different stitches. Now you're ready to start sewing like a real pro.

Use this sewing machine checklist every time you sit down to sew.

√ My sewing machine is plugged in and turned on.

√ My needle is properly threaded.

√ I've set the sewing machine to the type of stitch I want to use.

√ The tail ends of the threads are long enough to touch my sewing table.

√ My fabric is in position, and I've remembered to lower the presser foot before I begin to sew.

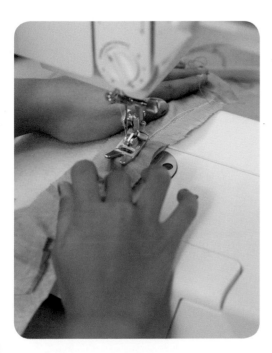

Position Your Fabric

With the presser foot up, slide your fabric onto the sewing machine bed so that most of the fabric is to the left of the needle. You'll want the top edge of the fabric just a tiny bit behind the needle and the right edge of the fabric lined up with the side of the presser foot.

The projects in this book are designed with ¼-inch seam allowances. The seam allowances refer to the space between your stitches and the edge of your fabric. No matter what kind of sewing machine you have, when the presser foot is correctly lined up with the fabric, it will create a standard seam allowance of ¼ inch.

Note: If some day you work with other patterns, they might be designed with ½-inch or ⅝-inch seam allowances, and most machines have lines marked on them that act as guides for those seam allowance widths.

Guide Your Fabric

Guiding fabric through a sewing machine is very different than holding fabric when you sew it by hand. First of all, even though you're sewing slowly, machines work much faster than your hands do. You have to be very careful

to keep your fingers far away from the sewing machine needle as it zips up and down.

1 Sit down with both feet flat on the floor. It never works to stand and sew! Make sure the machine is turned on. Place your fabric on the machine and use the lever to drop the presser foot. Gently rest the fingertips of both hands on the sides of the fabric that are between you and the machine.

2 Now put your right foot on the machine's foot pedal, and slowly start to sew. As the needle sews through the fabric, the rough-feeling feed dogs on the needle plate will gently pull the fabric through the machine.

3 Use your fingertips to gently help guide the fabric past the needle. The stitches will go wherever you guide the fabric.

> TIP: The seam allowance is the space between your stitches and the edge of your fabric. Most seam allowances are ¼ inch. Find the seam allowance guide on your machine's needle plate, and as you guide the fabric through the machine, keep it on that line.

Sew a Seam

 1 With the presser foot up, position the fabric.

 2 Use the lever to drop the presser foot, and use the straight stitch to sew a straight line down the edge of the fabric until you have about ½ inch of stitches.

3 Press the reverse knob or dial, and sew backward on the same line of stitches. Let go of the reverse control and sew forward again. Use your presser foot as a guide to keep your stitches where they need to be. If you veer too close to the edge of the fabric, or off the fabric altogether, the fabric will fray and your stitches will fall out!

4 Continue sewing until you reach the end of the fabric, and press reverse again to resew the final ½ inch of stitches.

5 Use the hand wheel to lift your needle, and use the lever to lift the presser foot. Gently pull your fabric off the sewing machine until your thread touches the table.

6 Carefully cut through both threads, and you're done! You have sewn a seam.

Every time you've finished sewing a seam, pause to trim the threads that hang off your fabric. Snip these threads short so they don't get tangled up when you start sewing

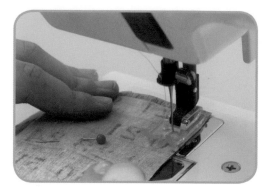

again. Keep a trash can near your sewing machine so cleanup is easy.

Note: Some modern sewing machines allow you to adjust the presser foot position. For the projects in this book, check your sewing machine manual to make sure that your presser foot is in the basic, middle position.

Reinforce Stitch

A reinforce stitch helps to make sure that a part of the project like a strap or loop will be strong and not come undone. Follow these three simple steps to add strength to your seams.

1 Sew forward over the area to be reinforced as normal. This might be a handle or elastic loop.

2 Once you are a little past the area, reverse stitch back over the area.

3 Sew forward over the area again and keep sewing the project according to the project directions.

That's it! Now your handles, straps, and elastic loops should hold on tight.

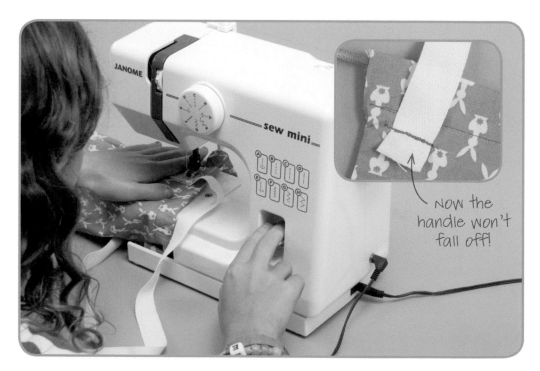

Now the handle won't fall off!

Turn a Corner

You will have to turn corners a lot when sewing! A nice, sharp corner will make your projects look neater and give them shape. Follow these steps and you'll be a master at corner turning.

"Put the needle down when you turn fabric at the corner!"
— MAXINE, 8

1 Be sure to keep your eye on the presser foot and stop sewing when the very front of the presser foot gets to the edge of the fabric at a corner.

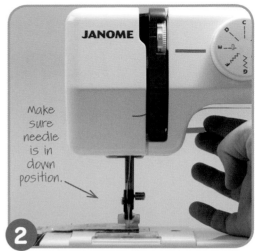

Make sure needle is in down position.

2 Make sure your needle is down in the fabric. If you need to, turn the hand wheel toward you until your needle is in the down position. Raise the presser foot by lifting the lever in the back of the machine.

3 Now the fabric can move around. Turn the corner by swinging the fabric toward you.

4 Put the presser foot back down by pushing down the lever.

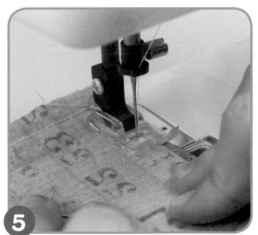

5 You turned a corner! Keep sewing happily along.

Turn the Good Side Out

Many of the projects in this book ask you to sew with the good sides together and then turn the good side out. This way, your project will look neat and professional. Plus, it won't fray. Once you know how to turn the good sides out, you can sew all kinds of things!

1

After tracing the pattern and cutting out the fabric, put the two pieces of fabric together, with the good sides touching.

2

Add a few straight pins so that the fabric layers stay together while you sew.

The fabric between the two lines will make an opening so you can turn the good side of the fabric out.

3

In the middle of one fabric edge, mark start and stop sewing lines with chalk; make the distance between the two lines about the same length as your index finger.

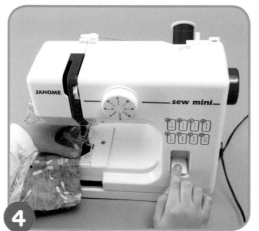

4

Begin to sew at the start sewing line. After sewing a few stitches, remember to reverse stitch.

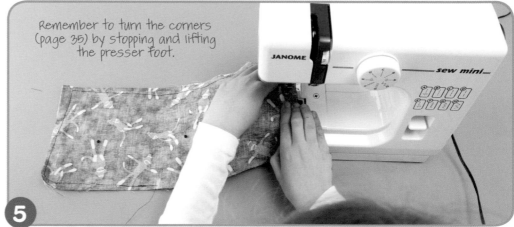

Remember to turn the corners (page 35) by stopping and lifting the presser foot.

5

Machine-stitch all the way around the fabric layers until you get to the stop sewing line. Remove the pins as you get to them and don't stitch over them. Reverse stitch at the stop stitching line. You should have an opening between the place you started sewing and where you stopped.

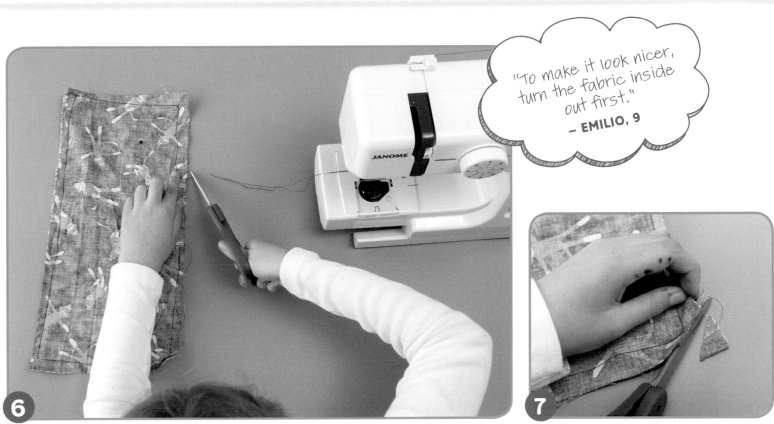

"To make it look nicer, turn the fabric inside out first."
— EMILIO, 9

6 Raise the presser foot and needle. Pull the fabric off the machine until the threads rest on the table. Now, cut the threads near the fabric.

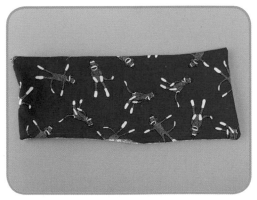

7 Carefully trim the pointy part of the corners. Do not cut the stitches! This helps the corners stick out better when you turn the good side out.

8 Remove any pins and turn the good sides out! Put your hand inside the opening and reach for the opposite side. Slowly pull the fabric out through the hole. This is like turning a sock right side out. Just keep working on it until it's all out.

9 To poke out corners or get into tight places, use the end of a pencil or a chopstick.

The good side is out and you are ready to continue your project.

Stuffing and Topstitching

Each project is different, but basic stuffing and topstitching techniques are easy. Refer to the project directions to see how to finish your project.

Stuffing

Some sewing projects, like pillows and dolls, need to be stuffed. You can buy stuffing at a fabric store or craft store. Use polyfill or your own stuffing to stuff your project.

you can also make your own stuffing using small fabric scraps that you might otherwise throw away.

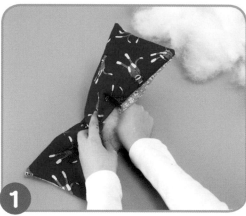

1 Stuff small handfuls into the opening and continue stuffing until you like the fluffiness of the project. Use a chopstick or the end of a pencil to stuff corners and small areas.

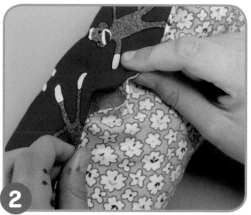

2 Once your project is stuffed, it's time to close it up. To do this, fold in the seam allowances at the opening.

3 Pin the opening closed.

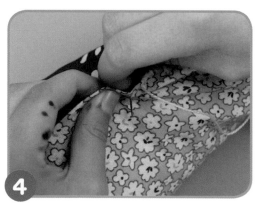

4 Don't try to use a sewing machine to close a stuffed project. You need to hand-sew the opening closed using a whipstitch (page 151).

All stuffed and sewn!

"match threads when you hand-sew after stuffing."
— MIRIAM, 8

Topstitch

You often topstitch items that aren't stuffed or use it as decorative stitching. Topstitching gives a project a professional and finished feeling.

1 Fold in the seam allowances at the opening.

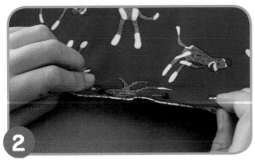

2 Pin the opening closed.

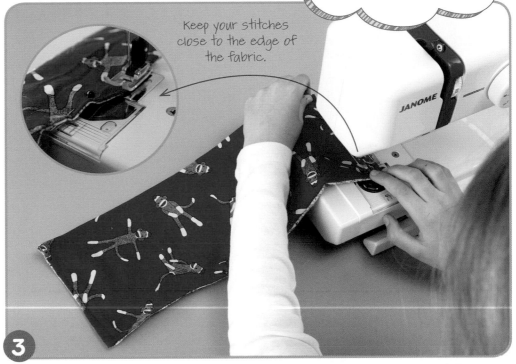

Keep your stitches close to the edge of the fabric.

3 Beginning a little before the opening, machine-sew all the way around the project. As you sew, keep your stitches close to the edge of the fabric and sew the opening closed. Start and stop stitching in the same place. When the stitching gets back around to your beginning stitches, reverse stitch.

4 Raise the presser foot and needle. Pull the fabric off the machine until the threads rest on the table. Now, cut the threads near the fabric.

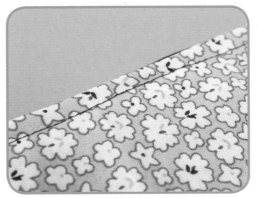

You made a topstitched project!

TIP: If the fabric is wrinkled, you can iron it flat before sewing.

Bring Your Project to Life

Every project in this book has basic sewing steps, but it's fun to "Make It Yours" by sewing on notions and trims. You might get some creative ideas from the pictures in this book, or you might dream up something completely new.

Make It Special

Here are some ways you can turn an ordinary sewing project into something unique.

* **Use iron-on patches** made for mending to create your own design. Cut shapes out of the patches with scissors. Then ask a grown-up to help with the ironing.

* Personalize your project with **press-on letters, fabric markers, or crayons**. Make a monogram with your initials, label your project with your name, or draw a picture directly on the fabric.

TIP: If you're using crayons, you'll want to set your image into the fabric before you begin to sew your project. Ask an adult to help you with this! Turn the iron to a high-temperature setting and then carefully place your fabric on the ironing board. Make sure the fabric is smooth. Cover it with a blank sheet of paper. Iron the paper for a few seconds, until the heat of the iron melts the crayon wax into the fabric. Let the fabric cool before you sew with it!

* **Embroidery** is another cool and beautiful way to create one-of-a-kind work. Usually you will need to embroider your fabric before you move to the sewing machine to put your project together. Draw your design on the fabric with a pencil or chalk. Then, embroider directly over the lines using a hand needle and craft thread and a running stitch. It's just like drawing with your needle!

Adding Trim

Buttons, ribbons, rickrack, fabric scraps, and other notions are an easy way to give some personality to your project! Use hook-and-loop tape (a popular brand is Velcro) in place of a button or zipper. Sometimes you need to hand-sew these notions onto your fabric pieces before you machine-stitch the project. Other times, you can add finishing touches at the end. Check out the Make It Yours section for each project to see when it's okay to stop following instructions and customize your work.

You usually need to attach your notions and trims with hand stitching. If you want your hand stitches to disappear, use a smaller needle and your regular sewing machine thread. Try to find a color of thread that matches your fabric, or a color that blends into the trim that you are adding to your project.

To decide which trims to use, experiment by laying a piece of ribbon or rickrack across the cut-out fabric pieces. Be sure to lay the trim on the outside, or good side, of the fabric. When you've found the perfect place to attach it, use pins to hold the trim to the fabric so it will stay in place while you sew. Carefully hand-sew running stitches down the middle of narrow trim. If the trim is wide, hand-sew running stitches down each side. Small stitches will help the trim to stay on better. See page 149 for hand-sewing stitches.

If you're careful, you can also use your sewing machine to attach trim to your fabric. Be sure to work slowly! Remove each pin as it gets close to the needle, and sew the trim from one edge of the fabric to the other edge. When you move on to the project steps, the rough ends of trim will be hidden in the seam allowance.

Pop Quiz

Put your skills to the test by making these sewing accessories. Once you have sewn them, you'll know you have what it takes to graduate to the other projects in this book.

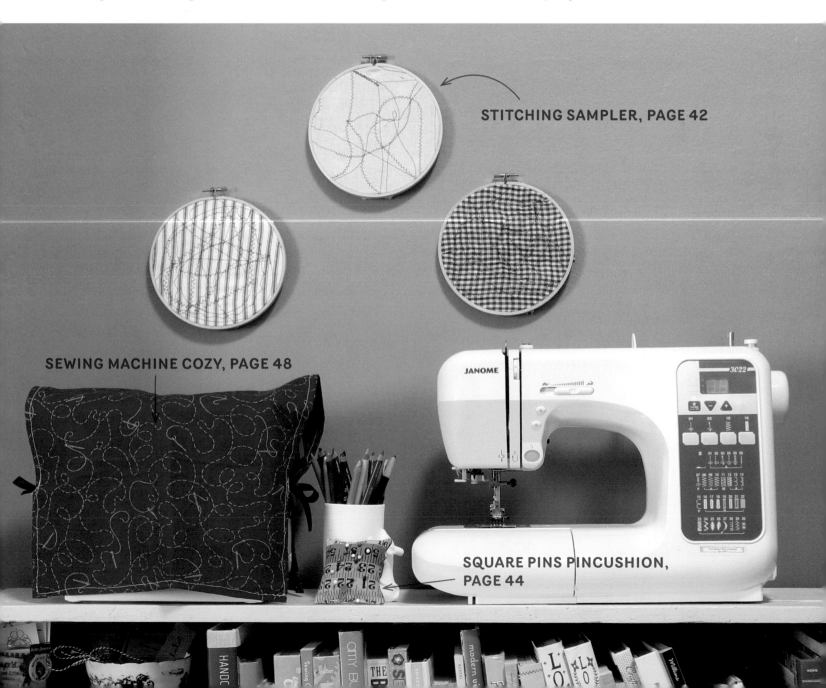

STITCHING SAMPLER, PAGE 42

SEWING MACHINE COZY, PAGE 48

SQUARE PINS PINCUSHION, PAGE 44

Stitching Sampler ☆

Learn to use your sewing machine while making a one-of-a-kind sampler.

What You Need

x Cotton fabric scraps about the size of a sheet of paper

x Scissors

x Sewing machine and thread

LET'S REVIEW

Turn a corner (page 35)

Sew in a circle (page 136)

A NOTE FOR GROWN-UPS

Making a sampler is a wonderful way to get acquainted with the sewing machine! After making a sampler or two, kids should have gained the confidence and skills needed to tackle the one-star projects in this book. Sit by your new sewer and talk him or her through the process. Try not to jump in too much because the goal here is independence. After a sampler is completed, find a place to display the work.

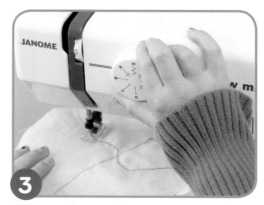

1 Make sure your needle is threaded and your bobbin is filled. Place your fabric on the machine and lower the presser foot.

2 Using both hands, slowly guide the fabric under the presser foot so that you are sewing in all different directions.

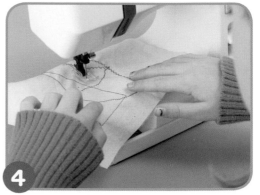

3 Change the stitches on your machine. Try them all and see how they look.

4 Practice turning corners. Make sure your needle is down in the fabric before you lift the presser foot and swing the fabric toward you. Directions for turning corners are on page 35.

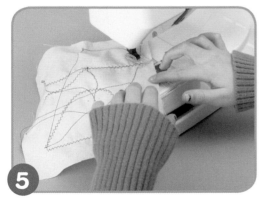

5 Guide the fabric around so you sew in a circle (page 136). You might want to try bringing your hands a little closer to make it easier.

6 Before you pull the fabric off the machine be sure to reverse stitch! Remember, you will reverse stitch every time you begin and stop sewing on a machine.

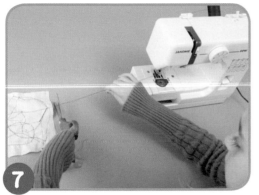

7 To pull your fabric off the machine, make sure your needle is up and then lift the presser foot lever. Gently pull, pull, pull the fabric off the machine until the loose threads hit the table.

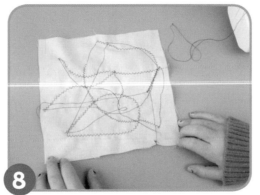

8 Cut the threads close to the fabric. You just made your first sewn work of art! What will you do with it? Can you find some pictures in it?

"Oh, look what I did! I see an angel!"
– GRACE, 9

Grace wanted to practice turning corners, so she sewed around the edges of her sampler.

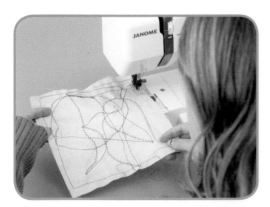

MAKE IT YOURS

* *Frame your sampler in an embroidery hoop and hang it on the wall to make instant artwork for your room!*

* *Sew it into a pillow or a purse.*

* *Change your thread colors and make a rainbow sampler.*

* *Cut your sampler into even squares to make drink coasters.*

* *Use it to wrap a special present for someone you love.*

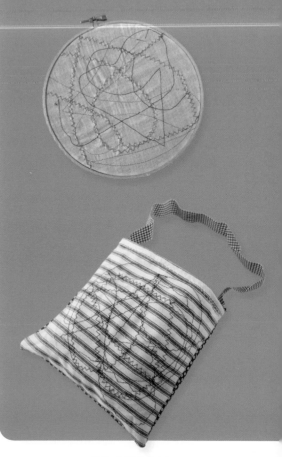

Square Pins Pincushion ☆

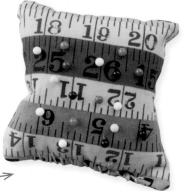

Keep your pins right where you need them with this handy pincushion.

What You Need

- x Pattern for Square Pins
- x Cotton fabric scraps at least 5 inches square
- x Stuffing
- x Chalk
- x Scissors
- x Straight pins
- x Hand sewing thread and needle
- x Sewing machine and thread

LET'S REVIEW

Turn a corner (page 35)

Turn the good side out (page 36)

Hand-sew a running stitch or whipstitch (page 151)

A NOTE FOR GROWN-UPS

This is a great first project. Sewers will learn how to turn corners, make a simple pillow, and practice using the sewing machine. First-time sewers may need help throughout the process.

"I've always wanted my own pincushion!"
— MAGGIE, 9

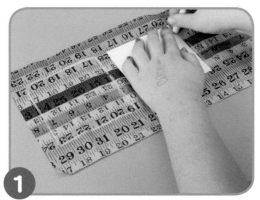

1 Find the Square Pins pattern piece in the back pocket. Use chalk to trace the pattern onto the fabric two times.

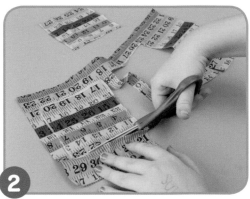

2 Cut out fabric.

3 Put the two pieces together with the good sides facing.

4 Add a pin in the center to hold them together.

mark start and stop lines.

5 In the middle of one side, mark two lines with chalk to show where to start and stop sewing. The space between the marks will make an opening in your pincushion so you can turn it good side out and stuff it.

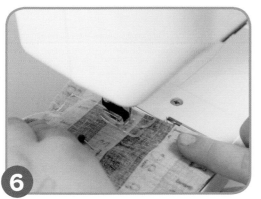

6 Begin sewing at the start sewing chalk mark with a reverse stitch. Sew around all sides, turning at the corners until you get to the stop sewing chalk mark. Reverse stitch at the end and pull the fabric off the machine.

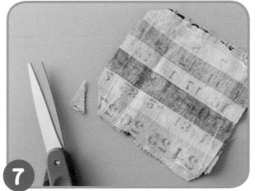

7 Trim all the loose threads from the fabric. Trim away the pointy corners, but be careful not to cut the threads.

GO TO NEXT PAGE →

MAKE IT YOURS

* *Use two different fabrics.*

* *Change the size or shape of the pincushion.*

* *Sew the pincushion by hand.*

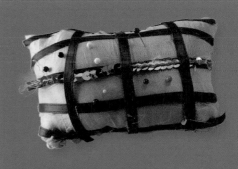

8

Turn the fabric good side out through the opening.

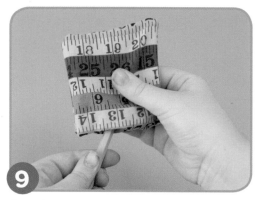

9

Gently push out the corners with the eraser end of a pencil if needed.

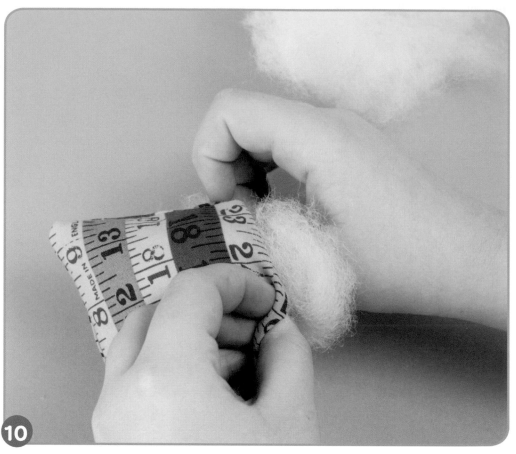

10

Stuff the pillow.

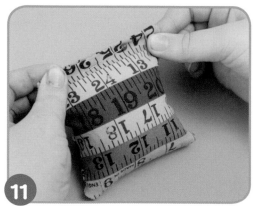

11

Time to close up the opening. Fold in the seam allowances at the opening and pin it closed.

12

Using a hand sewing needle and thread, sew the opening closed with a whipstitch.

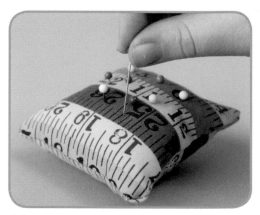

Add pins and put your new pincushion next to your sewing machine so you'll be ready for your next project!

PIN IT!

Pinning helps keep your fabrics together while you move it from the table to sewing machine. It also keeps the sides together while you sew. At first, pinning may seem a little tricky, but once you know how, it's easy-peasy.

We don't like to add a lot of pins unless we really need to. For most projects, simply add a pin or two away from the edge of the project and you can easily carry your project from a worktable to your sewing machine.

1 *Poke the point of the pin through both layers of fabric.*

2 *Gently squish up the fabric toward the ball end of the pin.*

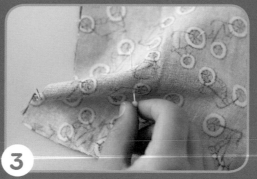

3 *Push the point of the pin up through the fabric.*

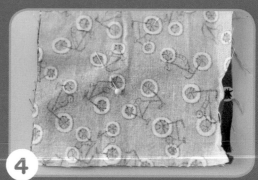

4 *The pin is in place!*

Sometimes, you might want to pin the edges of a project together.

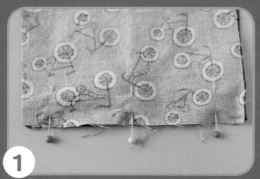

1 *Place pins along the edge a few inches apart. The ball end of the pins should always come off the edge so you can take them out easily as you sew along.*

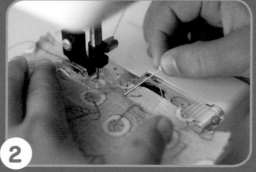

2 *When you come to a pin, take your foot off the pedal to stop sewing. Pull out the pin by the ball end.**

3 *It's nice to have a pincushion next to your sewing machine so the pins will have a place to go!*

*Never sew over a pin because it might break your needle.

Sewing Machine Cozy ☆

What You Need

- x Pattern for Sewing Machine Cozy that fits your sewing machine. Small pattern fits machines up to 9 x 11 inches; large pattern fits standard machines (about 12 x 15 inches)
- x Cotton fabric (½ yard for small, 1 yard for large)
- x 1¼ yards ribbon, at least ½ inch wide
- x Chalk
- x Scissors
- x Straight pins
- x Ruler
- x Iron and ironing board
- x Sewing machine and thread

Keep your sewing machine clean and ready with this simple case.

LET'S REVIEW

Turn a corner (page 35)

Machine-stitch a hem (page 50)

Reinforce stitch (page 34)

Iron safely (page 22)

Do you have a big or small machine? There's a pattern for both!

A NOTE FOR GROWN-UPS

A machine cozy is a must for any sewer because it protects the sewing machine from dust! This project practices essential skills such as turning corners and making a hem that are important to understand when making other projects in the book. Assist your child with ironing and talk about safety when sewing. Help may also be needed attaching the ties.

wrong side

right side

Place pattern on fold.

1 Find the Sewing Machine Cozy pattern piece that fits your machine in the back of the book. Fold the fabric in half so that the right sides are together, matching the selvages. Smooth out the fabric so there are no lumps.

2 Put the end of the pattern on the fold. Use chalk to trace the pattern onto the fabric one time.

3 Pin the fabric layers together and carefully cut along the chalk lines through both sides of the fabric. Do not cut the fold. After cutting, open the fabric. You will have one big piece of fabric.

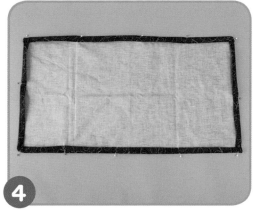

4 Time to make a hem. Follow the directions on page 50 for machine-stitching a ½-inch-wide hem all the way around the fabric.

MAKE IT YOURS

* *Add a pocket to the cozy.*

* *Decorate your cozy with trim or embroidery. Does your sewing machine have a name?*

* *Make a double-sided cozy by following the directions for Turn the Good Side Out (page 36). You won't need to hem a double-sided cozy.*

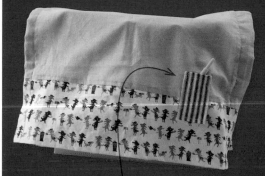

Add a pocket for your seam ripper!

Take the pins out as you sew.

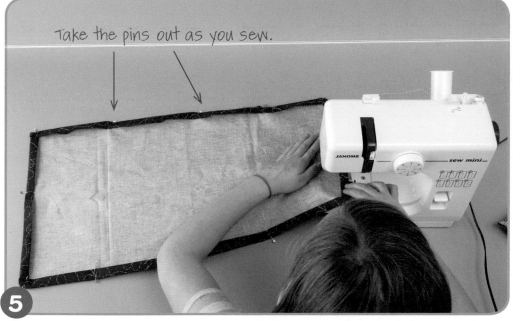

5 Once your hem is ironed and ready to sew, begin stitching in the middle of one side. Using the presser foot as your guide, sew around all four sides of the cozy. Take the pins out as you sew and go around the corners carefully. When you meet the beginning stitches, reverse stitch and pull the fabric off the machine.

GO TO NEXT PAGE

How to Machine-Stitch a Hem

A hem is a neat, turned-under edge that makes your sewing look professional. Making a hem requires the use of an iron, so ask a grown-up for help.

   To make a hem you will fold under the fabric two times. Iron the fabric each time. Follow the directions in the pattern for how wide to make the hem. This hem is ½ inch wide.

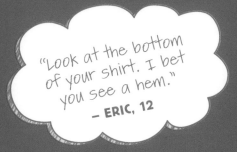

"Look at the bottom of your shirt. I bet you see a hem."
— ERIC, 12

1 Lay the fabric good side down. Fold over the edge of the fabric you want to hem ½ inch. You will see the good side folded over.

2 Iron down the fold. Repeat for all the edges you are hemming.

3 Now, fold the edge over again. The second fold is ½ inch again.

4 Iron the second fold. Repeat for all the edges that are being hemmed.

5 Pin down the folded hem so that it will stay put until you sew it.

6 Topstitch close to the inside folded edge.

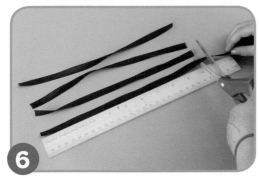

6

Cut four ribbons, each 10 inches long.

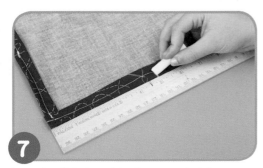

7

Lay the fabric with the good side down. Measure 5 inches across the hemmed edges from each corner for the small cozy and 6 inches for the large cozy. Mark the measurements with chalk.

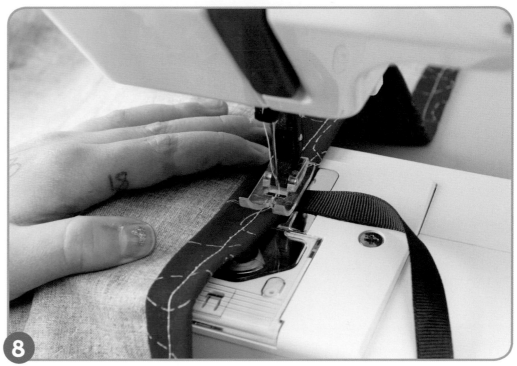

8

Lay the fabric with the good side down at the sewing machine and put the edge of one ribbon on a chalk mark. Sew a reinforce stitch on the ribbon by sewing across, reverse, and then across again. Do this for all four ribbons and chalk marks.

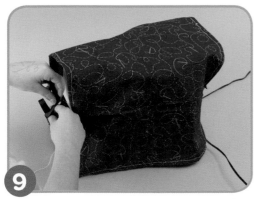

9

Lay the cozy over your machine and tie the ribbons. Your sewing machine is so cozy now!

"My sewing machine is my new best friend!"
– GRACE, 9

"I wonder what I should sew next..."
– ANNIE, 12

IN MY ROOM

Be an interior designer. Make your space your own by customizing the projects in this chapter. Think about your favorite colors and designs. Do you like elephants, flowers, or maybe hedgehogs? Perhaps your little brother needs something of his own so he'll stay out of your room.

☆ *easy*   ☆☆ *medium*   ☆☆☆ *hard*

Secret Message Pillow ☆

What You Need

- x Pattern for Secret Message Pillow
- x Pattern for Perfect Pocket
- x ½ yard cotton fabric
- x 1 felt square for pocket
- x Stuffing
- x Chalk
- x Scissors
- x Straight pins
- x Hand sewing needle and thread
- x Sewing machine and thread

LET'S REVIEW

Hand-sew a running stitch or whipstitch (page 151)

Turn the good side out (page 36)

Turn a corner (page 35)

A NOTE FOR GROWN-UPS

This pillow lends itself to many variations. Some sewers might need help sewing on the pocket. More experienced sewers should try following the Perfect Pocket directions (page 58).

This pillow has a little pocket that's just right for holding a secret message, or maybe a tooth!

Trace the pattern on the fabric two times.

1 Find the pattern for the Secret Message Pillow in the back of the book. With chalk, trace it onto your fabric two times.

2 Cut out the fabric.

3 Find the pattern for the Perfect Pocket in the back of the book. With chalk, trace it onto your piece of felt one time.

4 Cut out the felt pocket. Pin the pocket in the middle of one of the pillow pieces.

Don't forget to leave the top of your pocket open!

5 Machine-stitch the pocket onto the pillow. Start at the top right-hand corner and sew all three sides; turn the corners. Be sure to leave the top of the pocket open.

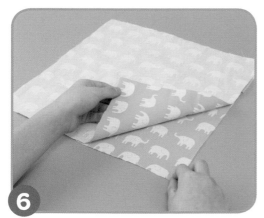

6 Put both pillow pieces together with the good sides facing. You can pin the pillow around the edges if you like.

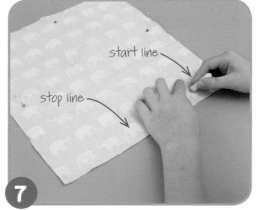

start line

stop line

7 With chalk, mark start and stop sewing lines on the bottom edge of the pillow. This will be the opening for turning the pillow right side out.

GO TO NEXT PAGE

"I like writing messages and then reading them again and again."
— **MAXINE, 9**

MAKE IT YOURS

* *Change the size or shape of the pillow. How about adding a pocket to both sides of the pillow?*

* *Add a cotton pocket. See the Perfect Pocket (page 58) for directions.*

* *Embellish the pillow with trims before sewing the two sides together. Maybe stitch on a secret message! You can add buttons once the sides are sewn together.*

* *Make an autograph pillow for your friends to sign when they come over to visit.*

* *Hand-sew the pillow.*

Add a button!

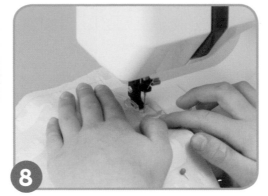

8 Beginning at the start sewing line, machine-stitch around the pillow; turn the corners. At the stop sewing line, reverse stitch and take the fabric off the machine.

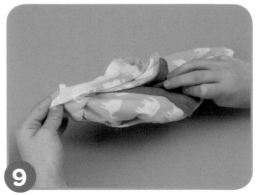

9 Clip off the seam allowances at the corners so they will be pointy. Turn the pillow good side out. Use a chopstick or end of a pencil to gently poke out the corners.

10 Stuff the pillow until it is full and fluffy.

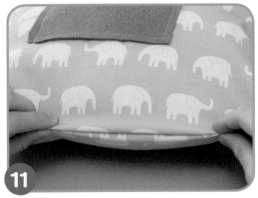

11 Fold in the seam allowances at the opening and pin closed.

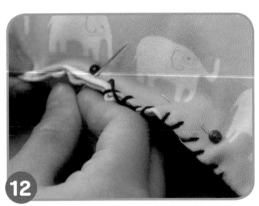

12 Hand-sew the opening closed with a whipstitch.

Add a secret message for a friend or maybe the tooth fairy!

Secret Code

After you finish making the Secret Message Pillow, you need to devise a code for your secret messages. One of our favorite codes is the Caesar Cipher. Devised by Julius Caesar, it's an easy-to-use encryption technique that will perplex your enemies or at least your little brother or sister. What you do is shift each letter of the alphabet down three places, so that your code looks like this.

plain alphabet	A	B	C	D	E	F	G	H	I	J	K	L	M	N	O	P	Q	R	S	T	U	V	W	X	Y	Z
code	C	D	E	F	G	H	I	J	K	L	M	N	O	P	Q	R	S	T	U	V	W	X	Y	Z	A	B

PQY OCMG C UGETGV OGUUCIG RKNNQY HQT C HTKGPF!

How to Make the Perfect Pocket

Sometimes you want the pocket to look professional with neat, turned-under edges. This pocket is made using cotton fabric. Ironing is needed as well, so ask a grown-up for help.

1 Find the Perfect Pocket pattern in the back of the book. Use chalk to trace the pattern onto cotton fabric one time. Cut out the fabric pocket.

¼" wide

2 Have an adult help you fold over and iron down the top edge two times. Make each fold ¼ inch wide.

3 Machine-stitch across the hem (see page 50).

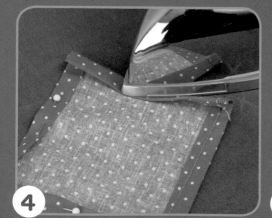

4 Now fold over and iron down the other three sides of the pocket about ½ inch. You only have to fold over and iron one time. Pin the folds down.

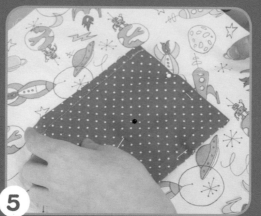

5 Put the pocket on the fabric, wherever you want it to be. Put the hemmed edge on the top. Move the pins from the wrong side of the pocket to the right side of the pocket so you can see them and the folds don't come out.

Sew the three sides of your pocket, but don't sew the top closed!

JANOME

6 Starting at the top right corner, machine-stitch around the three sides of the pocket. Turn the corners (page 35) and remove the pins as you sew. Don't sew the top, hemmed edge. You have a perfect pocket!

Welcome to My Room ☆

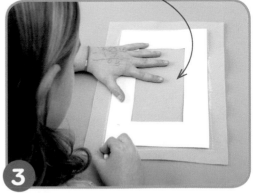

Tell everyone how you're feeling with this clever door sign that allows you to change the message.

"Sometimes I might use it to tell my sisters to stay out!"
– GRACE, 9

LET'S REVIEW

Turn a corner (page 35)

Reinforce stitch (page 34)

A NOTE FOR GROWN-UPS

This door sign is so handy that you might be requesting one of your own! The pattern is a little tricky, so help might be needed in making sure the window is cut out in the cotton fabric and not in the felt fabric. The felt backing helps make the sign hang straight. Remind your young sewer not to sew too far across the opening when sewing on the ribbon handle.

1

Remember to trace the opening for the window, too!

Find the Welcome to My Room pattern in the back of the book. Cut out the pattern and the window drawn on the pattern. Use chalk to trace the pattern onto cotton fabric one time. Trace the opening for the window onto the cotton fabric, too.

Don't trace the window this time!

Fold fabric in half and cut a slit.

2

Cut out the fabric. To cut the window opening, fold the fabric in half and cut a slit. Now you can easily get your scissors into the window to cut along the markings. You will have a piece of cotton fabric with a window inside of it.

3

Next, trace the Welcome to My Room pattern onto the felt fabric one time. This time, do not trace the window.

GO TO NEXT PAGE

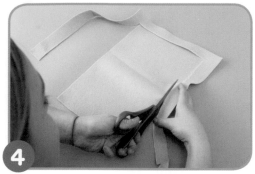

4 Cut out the felt piece around the outer edges. It should be a solid rectangle.

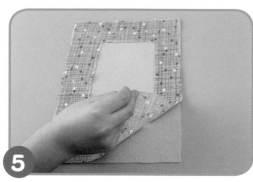

5 Put the cotton fabric on top of the felt fabric with both good sides facing up.

6 Starting at the top right corner, machine-stitch around the three sides. Leave the top open. Do not sew around the window.

MAKE IT YOURS

* *Change the size of the sign.*

* *Make the sign double-sided.*

* *Embellish with buttons and trims before you sew the sides together.*

* *Use your hand-sewing skills to embroider a message.*

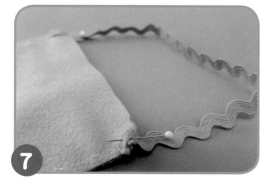

7 On the back, pin each end of the ribbon onto the top edges of the sign right at the seams.

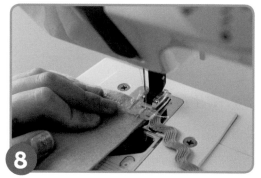

8 At the sewing machine, make a reinforce stitch on each end of the ribbon.

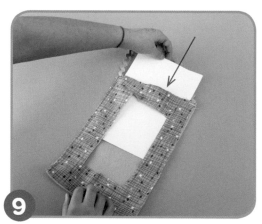

9 Fold the paper in half and slide it into the sign.

what will your sign say? you can change it whenever you need to!

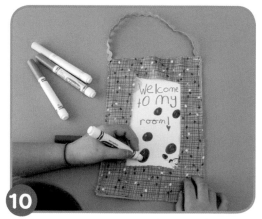

10 Write your message using markers or crayons in the window.

Sleepy Bear ☆☆

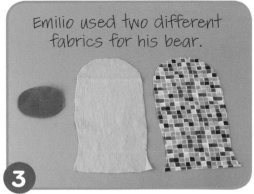

cuddle up with this super soft bear.
you get to design the shape of the ears!

What You Need

- x Pattern for Sleepy Bear
- x Pattern for Sleepy Bear Face
- x ¼ yard flannel fabric; you can use more than 1 color of fabric
- x Felt scraps for face
- x Stuffing
- x Chalk
- x Scissors
- x Straight pins
- x Ruler
- x Hand sewing needle and thread
- x Sewing machine and thread

LET'S REVIEW

Sew in a circle (page 136)

Hand-sew a running stitch or whipstitch (page 151)

Turn the good side out (page 36)

A NOTE FOR GROWN-UPS

Flannel fabric makes this bear extra cuddly and soft. Help may be needed guiding the sewing machine around the face and ear shape.

1 Find the patterns for the Sleepy Bear in the back of the book. Use chalk to trace the Sleepy Bear pattern onto flannel two times.

2 Use chalk to trace the Sleepy Bear Face pattern onto felt one time.

Emilio used two different fabrics for his bear.

3 Cut out all three pieces of fabric.

GO TO NEXT PAGE

"I might make a bear with just one big eye. That would be cool."
— EMILIO, 9

2 inches

4
Place the face piece onto the front of the Sleepy Bear at least 2 inches from the top. Pin it in place.

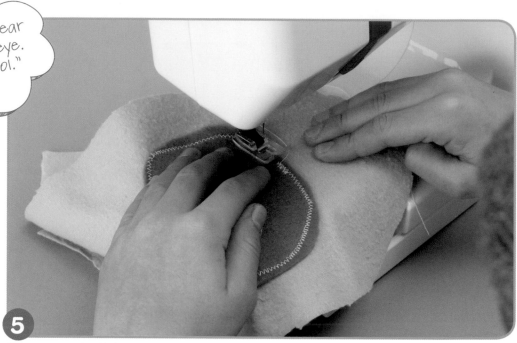

5
Zigzag stitch all the way around the edge of the face. Remember that when you sew around a curve, you don't stop and lift the presser foot.

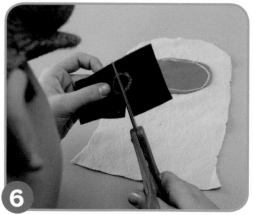

6
Design your bear's sleepy face. Draw and cut out a small, round nose from felt. Hand-sew the nose onto the face.

7
Using chalk, draw eyes and a mouth on your bear's face. Then, hand-sew along the chalk lines using a running stitch.

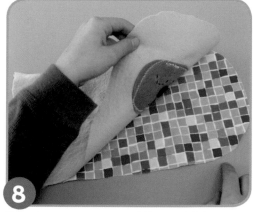

8
Put the two pieces of flannel fabric together with the good sides facing. Make sure the front of the bear is on top.

will the bear be smiling?

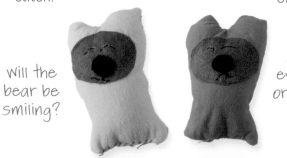

Are his eyes open or closed?

TURN THE PAGE

MAKE IT YOURS

* *Design the shape and size of your bear's ears.*

* *Change the size of the bear.*

* *Use cotton or felt fabric.*

* *Embellish the bear with buttons and trims.*

* *Leave the bottom open and you'll have a puppet!*

* *Hand-sew the bear.*

Add ribbons! →

Add arms!

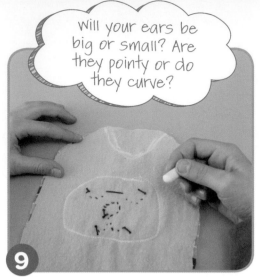

Will your ears be big or small? Are they pointy or do they curve?

9 Draw the ears of your Sleepy Bear with chalk. Be careful not to get too close to the bear's face.

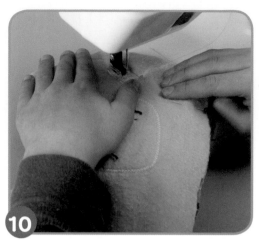

10 With chalk, mark a place to start and stop sewing on the bottom of the bear. Machine-stitch around the bear. When you get to the ears, guide the machine along your chalk line.

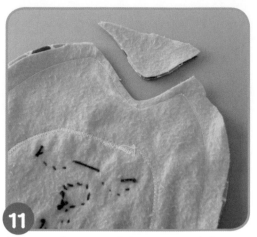

11 Cut out the extra fabric around the stitched ears. Be careful not to cut the threads.

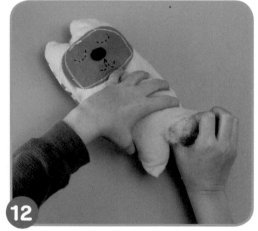

12 Turn the bear right side out. Stuff the bear. Be sure to get the stuffing into the ears. You want a soft and fluffy Sleepy Bear.

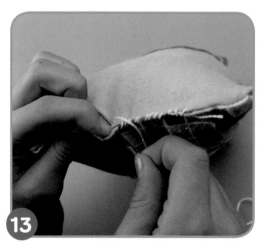

13 Fold in the seam allowances at the opening and pin closed. Hand-sew the opening closed using a whipstitch.

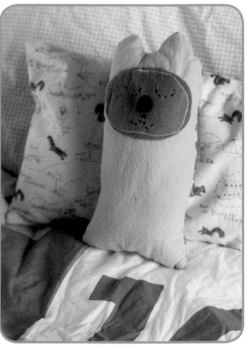

Give your Sleepy Bear a big hug and get ready for sweet dreams!

Wall Pocket ☆☆

What You Need

- Pattern for Wall Pocket
- Patterns for Wall Pocket Pockets (there are three different pocket sizes)
- Pattern for Wall Pocket Tab
- 1 yard cotton fabric
- Felt scraps for pockets and tabs
- Chalk
- Scissors
- Straight pins
- Sewing machine and thread

LET'S REVIEW

Turn a corner (page 35)

Reinforce stitch (page 34)

Turn the good side out (page 36)

A NOTE FOR GROWN-UPS

This large-scale wall hanging is perfect for sewers who have made several projects. Help may be needed sewing on the pockets and turning the fabric good side out.

This is the perfect place to stash your stuff. The best part? You get to decide how to design the pocket layout.

GETTING STARTED

Fold in half.

1 Fold the cotton fabric in half.

2 Find the Wall Pocket pattern in the back of the book and use chalk to trace it onto the fabric one time.

After cutting you will have two pieces.

3 Pin the fabric layers together and cut out along the chalk lines. After cutting, you will have two pieces of fabric.

GO TO NEXT PAGE

"It's perfect for holding my hairbrush and makeup."
— ANNIE, 12

MAKE THE POCKETS

1

Annie cut out 6 pockets, each from a different color of felt.

Time to make the Wall Pocket pockets. There are three different pocket pattern sizes in the back of the book to choose from. Decide what sizes and how many of each kind of pocket you want. Once you decide what to do, trace the pocket patterns onto felt and cut them out.

2

Arrange the pockets on one piece of fabric.

3

Pin down the pockets in place and carefully take your fabric to the sewing machine.

GO TO NEXT PAGE →

MAKE IT YOURS

* *Change the size of the wall pocket.*

* *Use chalkboard fabric so you can label the pockets.*

* *Make the pockets with cotton fabric. Look at Perfect Pocket for how-to, page 58.*

* *Use a dowel or curtain rod to hang up your Wall Pocket.*

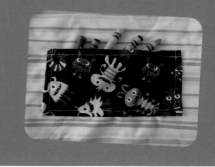

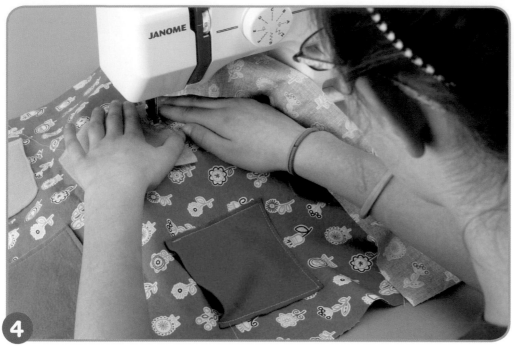

4

TIP: When you are sewing around the pockets, keep the fabric as flat as possible on top of the needle plate. If you aren't careful, the fabric will get bunched up under the presser foot and you might sew the wrong part of the fabric.

Starting at the top right corner, sew around three sides of each pocket. Be sure to leave the top of the pocket open! After sewing on a pocket, take the fabric off of the machine and cut the threads. Then, sew on the other pockets until they are all sewn onto the fabric. Trim all the loose threads.

5

Lay out the fabric with the pockets and put the other piece of fabric on top of it with the good sides together. Pin around the edges of the fabric.

6

With chalk, mark a 6-inch opening to start and stop sewing in the middle of a short end of the fabric. Start sewing at the starting point and sew all around the fabric until you get to the stop sewing mark.

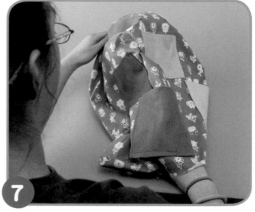

7

Clip away the corners of the fabric, being careful not to cut the stitches. Turn the fabric good side out through the opening.

ADD THE TABS

1 Now it's time to make the tabs so you can hang up your Wall Pocket. Trace the Wall Pocket Tab pattern onto felt three times. Cut out the tabs.

2 Fold the tabs in half and pin them onto the top part of the Wall Pocket. Place one in the middle of the top edge and the others about an inch from each side edge.

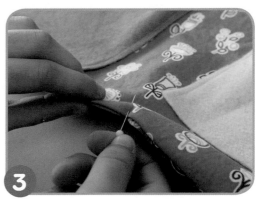

3 Find the opening in your Wall Pocket. Fold in the seam allowances at the opening and pin them closed.

4 Topstitch the Wall Pocket all the way around the edge of the fabric. When you get to the tabs, reinforce the stitches by going back and forth over the tabs.

Hang up your Wall Pocket and fill it with your favorite things.

Stripy Quilt ☆☆☆

What You Need

- ✗ 1 yard cotton fabric for the backing
- ✗ Four ¼-yard cuts of fabric for the patchwork top. Cut the fabric 9 inches long and from selvage to selvage
- ✗ 1 yard of batting, low or medium loft
- ✗ Lightweight yarn or craft thread
- ✗ Chalk
- ✗ Scissors
- ✗ Straight pins
- ✗ Ruler
- ✗ Iron and ironing board
- ✗ Hand sewing needle
- ✗ Sewing machine and thread

This tie-quilted throw will keep you cozy while you read a book or watch a movie.

LET'S REVIEW

Turn a corner (page 35)

Turn the good side out (page 36)

Iron safely (page 22)

A NOTE FOR GROWN-UPS

While simple in its construction, this quilt takes time to make. Keeping the fabric flat while sewing can be problematic for young sewers. The layers of the quilt are quite thick and might be hard to sew with a smaller machine. Due to the similar design, the eHold bag (page 94) is a good project to complete before making the quilt.

MAKE THE TOP

1 Lay out the four ¼-yard strips of fabric in the order you like. Stack the strips in order.

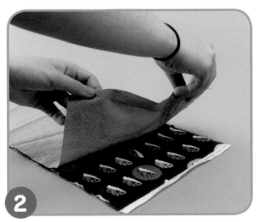

2 Pin the first two strips together with the good sides together. Pin along one long edge.

TIP: Place the pins about 6 inches apart.

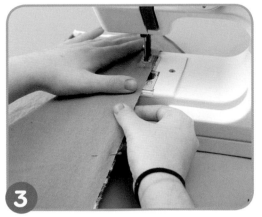

3 Machine-stitch along the pinned edge. Stop sewing and remove the pins along the way.

GO TO NEXT PAGE

Batting

Some projects in this book, such as the eHold and the Stripy Quilt, require batting. Batting is soft insulation that has been pressed into a thin sheet. You can measure and cut it like fabric. When you sew batting into a project, it makes the fabric that surrounds it warmer and adds a layer of soft protection. Think of batting as the marshmallow layer in s'mores.

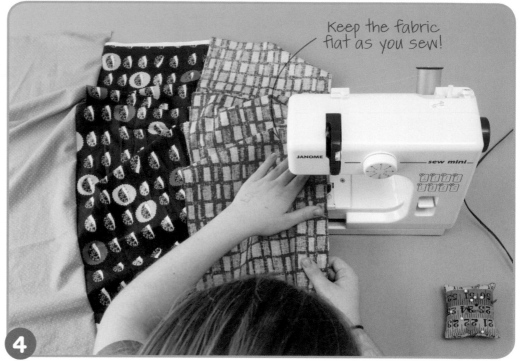

keep the fabric flat as you sew!

4 Add the remaining strips the same way. Pin the good side of each new strip to the last one sewn. When sewing, be careful to keep the fabric flat so that you won't accidentally sew the wrong parts of the fabric.

ADD THE BATTING

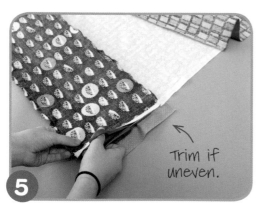

Trim if uneven.

5 Once the strips are sewn together you've made the top of the quilt! If the unstitched sides are uneven, trim them so they are all the same length.

6 Turn the top of the quilt over. Ask a grown-up to help you iron the seams flat.

1 It's time to prepare the other two layers of your quilt. Lay the batting down flat. Smooth the yard of backing fabric onto the batting with the good side facing up.

TIP: If the backing fabric has wrinkles or folds, ask a grown-up to help you iron it first.

"It takes a long time to make a quilt."
— FRANKIE, 7

2 Using the backing fabric as a guide, cut the batting around the fabric.

From top to bottom:
stripy top
backing fabric
batting

3 Lay the stripy top of the quilt on top of the backing fabric so the good sides are together. Take your time to match up the edges and make all the pieces as even as possible. Pin the layers together around the edge and in the middle of the quilt.

Mark start and stop lines.

4 In the middle of one edge, mark start and stop sewing lines with chalk around 9 inches apart so that the opening is big enough to turn the quilt good side out.

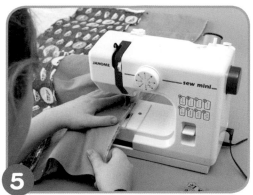

5 Carefully carry the quilt to the sewing machine. Beginning at the start sewing mark, machine-stitch around the edge of the quilt. Turn the corners and remove the pins as you go. Move the quilt slowly so that you don't poke yourself with a pin or shift the fabric layers.

6 Take out any remaining pins. Lay the quilt flat and cut the corners. You can also trim off any extra fabric or batting. You want the sides of the quilt to be even.

7 Time to turn the quilt good side out! Put your hand in the opening between the top and bottom layers of fabric and reach for the far corners. Grab them and pull them out through the opening. Keep pulling and turning the quilt until the good side is out and the batting is in the middle of the quilt.

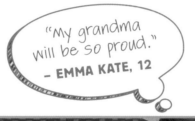

"My grandma will be so proud."
– EMMA KATE, 12

8 Fold in the seam allowances at the opening and pin them closed. If the quilt is bumpy, ask a grown-up to help you iron the entire quilt so it lies flat.

9 Position the quilt at your sewing machine with the stripy side facing up. Topstitch around all the edges of the quilt and close the opening as you sew. Be sure that the quilt is lying flat and the edge of your presser foot is going along the edge of the quilt.

TIE THE QUILT

1 Take the quilt off the sewing machine. With chalk and a ruler, mark the places to put the ties. Along the stripy edge, make a chalk mark in the middle of each stripe 2½ inches from the stitched edge.

2 Make marks in the center of each strip every 6 inches. Now it's time to tie the quilt.

When you tie your quilt, it will hold the three layers together and make it soft and quilted.

3 Tie your quilt! This is easiest to do while sitting on the floor or at a large table. Thread a hand sewing needle with a long strand of thin yarn or craft thread. Do not tie a knot at the end of the thread.

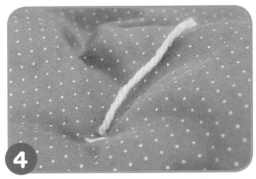

4 At a chalk mark, bring the needle down through all the layers of the quilt. Leave about a 2-inch-long tail.

5 Now, make a small running stitch by pushing the needle back up through the quilt. Push the needle up on the other side of the chalk mark on the top of the quilt.

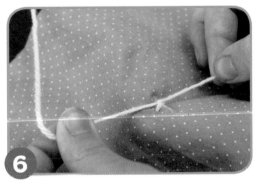

6 Tie the yarn ends together into a tight knot.

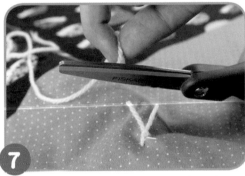

7 Trim the yarn ends to about ½ inch.

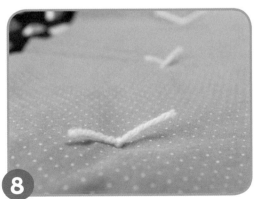

8 Continue making ties at each chalk mark. The middle sections can be a bit tricky to tie. If you want, fold up the sides of the quilt, so you can reach the area you are tying better.

Time to snuggle with your quilt!

MAKE IT YOURS

* *Make the strips of fabric skinnier or fatter.*

* *Finish the edges with bias tape.*

* *Use flannel fabric for a cozy quilt.*

* *Make a lighter-weight coverlet by skipping the batting.*

* *Go simple by quilting together 2 yards of your favorite fabric.*

* *Once you have made a Stripy Quilt, you can design your own quilt!*

Finish the edges →

"I always know which bag is mine!"
— CAROLINE, 11

LET'S GO

You are busy, always going from here to there. The projects in this chapter will help you keep track of all the things you need while on the road, from saving money, to going on a sleepover, to holding supplies.

☆ *easy*   ☆☆ *medium*   ☆☆☆ *hard*

"I like helping my mom cook at home. chocolate chip cookies are the best."
— MERIWETHER, 8

Cookie Coin Saver ☆

What You Need

- x Pattern for Cookie Coin Saver
- x 1 felt square for the cookie
- x Felt scraps for decoration
- x 1½-inch-length of stick-on hook-and-loop tape
- x Chalk
- x Scissors
- x Straight pins
- x Hand sewing needle and thread
- x Sewing machine and thread

LET'S REVIEW

Sew in a circle (page 136)

Hand-sew a running stitch or whipstitch (page 151)

A NOTE FOR GROWN-UPS

This little coin saver sews up quickly and easily. Your sewer might only need a bit of help decorating the cookie and sewing in a circle.

Save up for a yummy treat with this little coin saver that looks almost good enough to eat!

1 Find the pattern in the back of the book and use chalk to trace it onto felt two times.

2 Cut out the felt.

Anna decided to make her favorite, chocolate chip!

3 Time to decorate! You can make whatever kind of cookie you want. If you want chocolate chips, cut out little chips from felt.

MAKE IT YOURS

* *What kind of cookie do you want? The possibilities are endless!*

* *Close it with a button.*

* *You can fill the cookie with anything you want like earbuds, small toys, or lip balm.*

* *Stuff your cookie and make a little toy or pincushion.*

* *Use the pattern for the Superstar Microphone top and make a giant cookie for a purse or pillow.*

* *Sew the cookies by hand.*

Make a necklace!

Add a button!

4 Hand-sew the chips onto the felt cookie pieces.

Make short straight stitches on the tiny felt pieces and longer stitches on the back.

5 The trick is to keep sewing the chips on and don't knot off until you are done!

Mark start and stop sewing places

6 Pin the decorated cookies together with the good sides facing out. With chalk, mark a stop and start sewing place, about 1½ inches apart. This will be the top of the cookie.

7

Machine-stitch around the cookie.

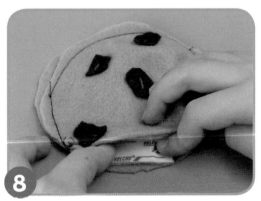

8

At the top opening, stick the hook-and-loop tape on one side at a time. Press down hard so both sides stick.

Saving money has never been so sweet!

Make a Cream-filled Cookie

Make white filling piece a little larger.

Use pinking shears to cut the outside cookie pieces for a fancy edge.

1

You will need scraps of black and white felt. Use the Cookie Coin Saver pattern to trace and cut two outside cookie pieces of black felt. Draw one filling piece a little larger than the outside cookie piece and cut it out of white felt.

2

Pin one outside cookie and the filling together. Machine-stitch all the way around the edges.

3

Pin the other outside cookie to the filling. With chalk, mark a stop and start sewing place, about 1½ inches apart.

4

Read Steps 7 and 8 for the Cookie Coin Saver to finish the cookie.

Tag Along ☆

Use your favorite fabric to create a little buddy to tag along with you wherever you go.

What You Need

- x Cotton fabric, printed with images or decorative motifs
- x Different cotton fabric for backing
- x Zipper hook, carabineer, key chain, or other kind of hook to attach to the Tag Along

- x Ribbon, 6 inches long
- x Stuffing
- x Scissors
- x Chalk
- x Straight pins
- x Hand sewing needle and thread
- x Sewing machine and thread

LET'S REVIEW

Hand-sew a running stitch or whipstitch (page 151)

Sew in a circle (page 136)

Turn a corner (page 35)

A NOTE FOR GROWN-UPS

This project is a fun way to use small leftover bits of a favorite fabric. If the motif or image on the fabric is small, it might be difficult to stuff and sew. You might need to help hand-sew the carabineer or hook onto the Tag Along.

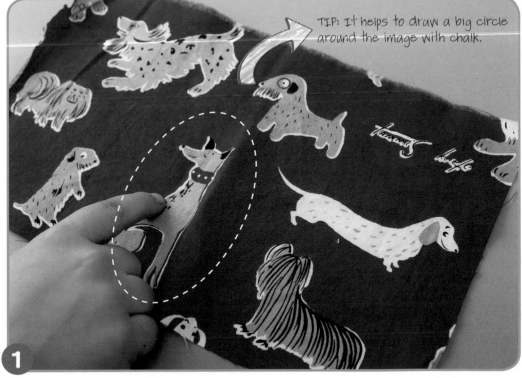

TIP: It helps to draw a big circle around the image with chalk.

1 Find an image on your fabric. Make sure it's not too small or you might have difficulty sewing it.

2 Cut out the image and leave a lot of space all around it; you might even cut into another image. That's okay.

3 Lay the image on top of your backing fabric with the good sides of both fabrics facing out. Pin the image in place.

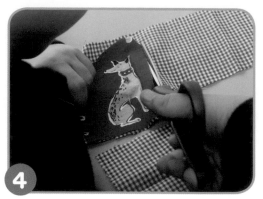

4 Use your image as a pattern to cut out the backing fabric. Chalk mark start and stop sewing marks at the bottom of the image.

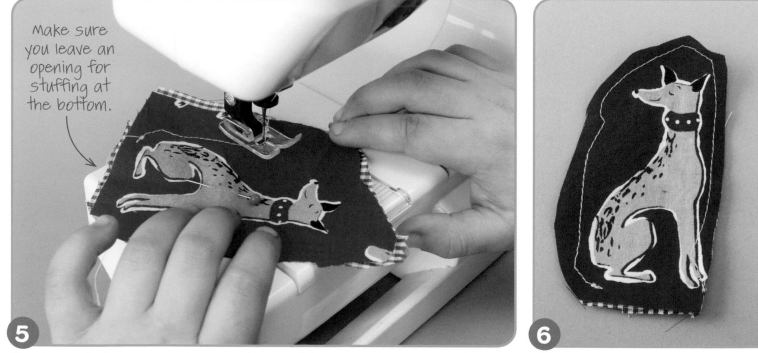

Make sure you leave an opening for stuffing at the bottom.

5 Starting at the bottom, machine-stitch around the image, leaving a small border of fabric all around. Make sure you leave an opening for stuffing at the bottom.

6 Cut off the extra fabric, close to the stitching, but don't cut your stitches!

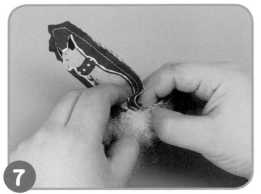

7 Stuff your Tag Along.

8 Hand-sew the bottom closed with a whipstitch.

9 You can use ribbon to attach the hook to the Tag Along. Fold the ribbon in half and sew the ends of the ribbon onto the back and top of the Tag Along with a few straight stitches. Then attach the hook to the ribbon.

TIP: You can also hand-sew the hook onto the Tag Along without using ribbon.

Where will you take your Tag Along?

MAKE IT YOURS

* *Leave the bottom open and you have a finger puppet.*

* *Add a string at the top and make a tree ornament.*

* *Sew several and hang them on a mobile.*

* *Sew by hand.*

"I like to draw when I'm waiting for my Mom."

— MAEVE, 8

Art-to-Go-Go ☆☆

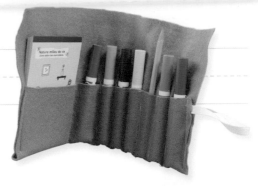

What You Need

- x Pattern for Art-to-Go-Go
- x ½ yard felt
- x 8-inch length of ¾-inch-wide elastic
- x Chalk
- x Scissors
- x Straight pins
- x Ruler
- x Sewing machine and thread

LET'S REVIEW

Turn a corner (page 35)

Reinforce stitch (page 34)

A NOTE FOR GROWN-UPS

This little art case is a fun beginner project. Sewers can customize it to hold all of their favorite supplies. Help might be needed when adding the elastic and marking and sewing the pockets.

Here's something to do when you're on the go-go.

1 Find the Art-to-Go-Go pattern in the back of the book and use chalk to trace it onto the felt one time.

2 Cut out the felt piece.

Fold fabric up to line.

3 Line up the felt piece with the pattern. Fold the bottom edge of the felt up, so the bottom of the folded felt is at the fold line.

4 Fold the piece of elastic in half. Tuck the ends of the elastic between the folds of the felt on the right side. Pin them in place.

5 Time to sew! Sew the right side closed, starting at the top near the elastic. When you get to the elastic, be sure to reinforce the stitches by going back and forth over the ends.

6 Sew up the other side of the fold. This time begin sewing at the bottom of the fold.

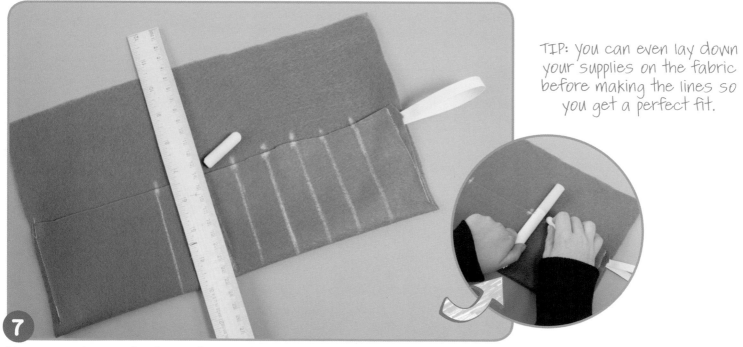

TIP: You can even lay down your supplies on the fabric before making the lines so you get a perfect fit.

7 You are ready to make the pockets on the folded part. Think about what you will put in your pockets. Draw lines using chalk and a ruler where you want the pockets to be. Make your pockets a little bigger than the markers or other items that will go in them. This way, the supplies will slide easily in and out of the pockets.

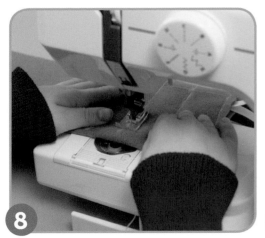

8 Machine-stitch along the chalk lines.

9 Trim the threads.

MAKE IT YOURS

* *Change the size of the case and pockets to fit your needs. A skinnier case is perfect for holding crayons.*

* *Make it out of two pieces of cotton fabric using the steps in Turn the Good Side Out (page 36) to get you started.*

* *Decorate the outside so everyone will know that it's yours.*

* *Sew by hand.*

* *A washcloth is perfect for holding your toothbrush.*

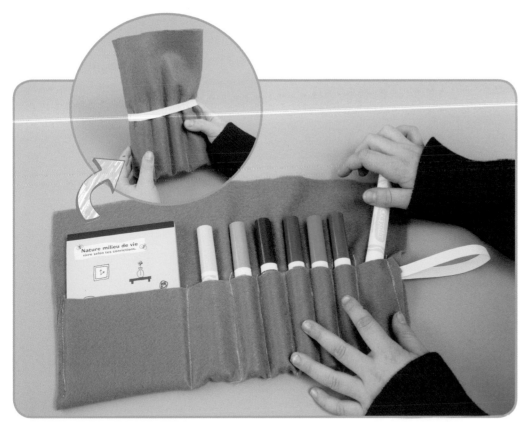

Your Art-to-Go-Go is all sewn. Fill it with your favorite art supplies, roll up, and go-go!

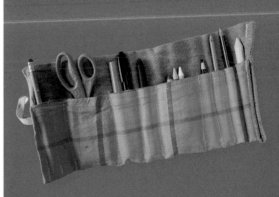

Zippy Pouch ☆☆

Zip up everything you need in this handy pouch.

What You Need

- x Pattern for Zippy Pouch
- x ¼ yard cotton fabric
- x 7-inch-long zipper
- x Chalk
- x Scissors
- x Straight pins
- x Hand sewing needle and thread
- x Sewing machine and thread

LET'S REVIEW

Turn a corner (page 35)

Hand-sew a running stitch or whipstitch (page 151)

A NOTE FOR GROWN-UPS

Zippers are fun but can be a bit tricky. In this project, we show how to hand-sew a zipper onto the pouch. Once a sewer understands how a zipper is attached, sewing it on by machine may be an option. If your child's machine has a zipper foot, your sewing machine manual should have directions for using it.

1 Find the pattern in the back of the book and use chalk to trace it onto the fabric two times. Cut out the fabric.

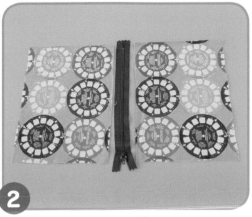

2 Lay the two pieces of fabric so that the good sides are facing up and the zipper is in the middle of two longer edges. The zipper is facing up too.

3 Flip one fabric piece over onto the zipper. Match the edge of the fabric to the edge of the zipper. Pin the fabric to the zipper. The zipper will extend beyond the fabric on each end.

4 Hand-sew the zipper to the fabric with a running stitch.

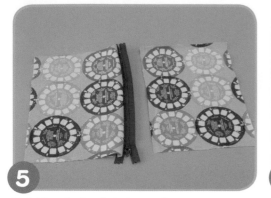

5 Fold back the fabric so that you see the top of the zipper. Press the fold with your fingers. With good sides up, line up the other piece of fabric with the zipper.

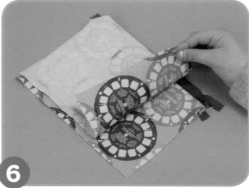

6 Flip the unsewn piece of fabric over. Match the edge of the fabric to the edge of the zipper that has not been sewn yet. Pin the fabric to the zipper like in step 3.

7 Hand-sew the zipper to the fabric with a running stitch like in step 4.

8 Fold back the fabric so you see the top of the zipper, and finger-press. Both pieces of fabric are sewn to the zipper. Unzip the zipper halfway so that you can turn the pouch good side out after sewing it with the machine.

"Keep the zipper open a little when you sew the bag."
— CATE, 10

9 Fold the pouch at the zipper so the good sides are together. Pinch the ends of the zipper together and pin them in place. Put a pin in the middle of the fabric so the sides don't move while you sew.

Be careful to only sew on the fabric part of the zipper, not the metal part, or your needle will break!

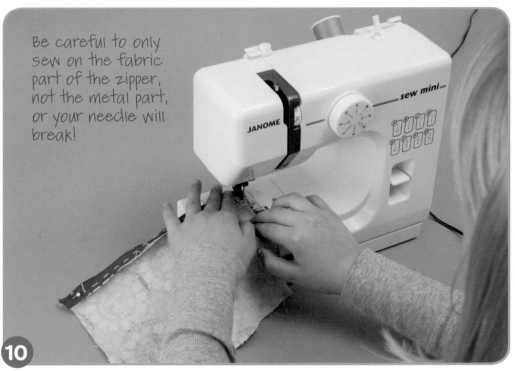

10

Beginning at the top, machine-stitch the three open sides of the pouch. You will sew through the ends of the zipper on both sides of the pouch; reverse stitch at the beginning and end. Turn the corners carefully.

11

Clip the corners of the seam allowances. If the ends of the zipper are long, trim them near the sewn edge. Turn the pouch good side out through the open zipper.

Fill your pouch and zip up!

MAKE IT YOURS

* *Change the size of the pouch to fit your needs. Make sure your zipper is long enough to fit the new size.*

* *Make each side with a different fabric.*

* *Add a handle for a smart clutch.*

* *Sew by hand.*

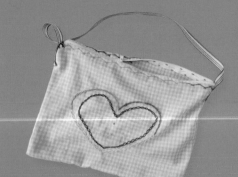

Decorate with embroidery!

eHold ☆☆☆

What You Need

- x Pattern for eHold
- x Pattern for eHold Pocket
- x ½ yard cotton fabric for outside
- x ½ yard cotton fabric for inside
- x ¼ yard for pocket
- x ½ yard medium- or low-loft batting (page 72)
- x 1 yard of 1-inch-wide ribbon
- x Chalk
- x Scissors
- x Straight pins
- x Ruler
- x Iron and ironing board
- x Sewing machine and thread

A messenger-style padded bag to keep your electronics safe and cozy. There's even a pocket for little things.

LET'S REVIEW

Reinforce stitch (page 34)

Sew a perfect pocket (page 58)

Iron safely (page 22)

Turn the good side out (page 36)

Machine-stitch a hem (page 50)

Turn a corner (page 35)

A NOTE FOR GROWN-UPS

The construction of this bag may be challenging for some sewers, especially when sewing in the batting. When sewing up the sides, help might be needed keeping the handles in place. A larger style sewing machine makes sewing up the sides much easier.

GET STARTED

1 Fold the outside fabric in half. Find the eHold pattern for the bag in the back of the book. Place the bottom of the pattern along the fold of the fabric. Use chalk to trace the pattern onto the fabric one time.

2 Pin the fabric layers together so they don't shift while you cut. Cut out the fabric. Do not cut the fold. You will have one piece of fabric.

TURN THE PAGE

"I love this bag!"
— ANNA MERCEDES, 10

MAKE IT YOURS

* Sew lines down the pocket to make a lot of smaller pockets.

* Make a pocket on the outside of the bag too.

* Don't add batting and make a simple, lined messenger-style bag.

* Go super simple by using just one piece of felt.

POCKET TIME!

3 Repeat steps 1 and 2 with the inside fabric.

4 Now, find the eHold Pocket pattern in the back of the book. Use chalk to trace the pocket onto your pocket fabric one time.

5 Cut out the pocket.

6 Hem the top of the pocket along one long side (page 50). To machine-stitch the hem, fold the edge ½ inch to the wrong side two times and iron it in place.

7 Machine-stitch the top hem of the pocket.

8 Fold the bottom of the pocket ½ inch to the wrong side and iron it flat.

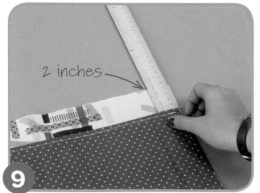

2 inches

9 Pin the pocket onto the outside fabric about 2 inches down from the top. Be sure that the hemmed edge of the pocket is at the top.

10 Sew around the three sides of the pocket, but leave the top edge open. Turn corners. When you sew across the bottom fold, be sure to keep the pocket flat so that you don't sew the wrong part.

ADD BATTING

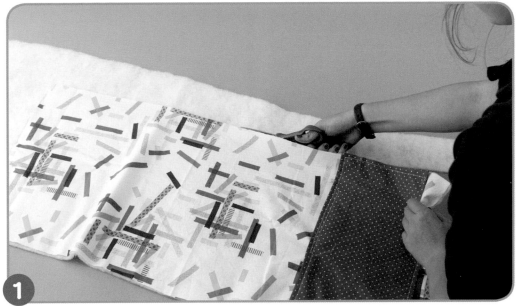

1 Lay the outside fabric on top of the batting with the good side up. Use the fabric as a pattern to carefully cut out the batting around the fabric.

The order of the three layers from the top to the bottom should be outside fabric, inside fabric, batting.

2 Put the inside fabric on top of the outside fabric with the good sides together.

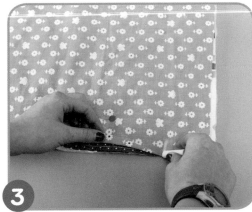

3 Pin all three layers together. Find a side where the pocket is sewn. With chalk, mark start and stop lines along the side. The marks should be about 5 inches apart.

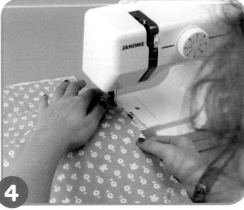

4 Machine-stitch around all the sides beginning and ending at the chalk marks. Stitch slowly, making sure you are sewing through all three layers and turn the corners. Clip the corners and trim off any extra batting or fabric.

5 Turn the bag good side out by reaching through the opening between the two layers of fabric. The batting will come out too and end up in the middle. You might need to push out the corners with the end of a chopstick or pencil.

TIP: If the fabric is wrinkled when it comes out, you can iron it flat.

ATTACH THE HANDLE

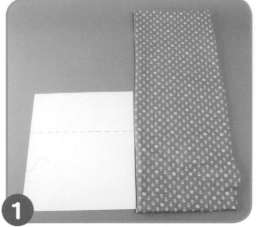

1 Lay the eHold next to the eHold pattern with the inside fabric facing up. Position the bottom of the pattern next to the bottom of the eHold.

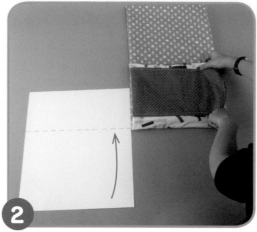

2 Fold the bottom of the eHold up at the dotted fold line.

If the pocket doesn't show, fold the eHold up a bit more.

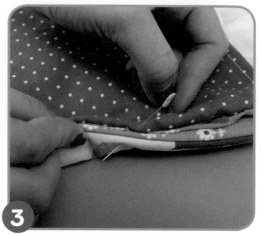

3 Find the opening that you made on one side. Fold in the seam allowances and pin them in place.

4 Pin the ends of the ribbon at the top of the fold to make the strap. Be careful not to twist the ribbon.

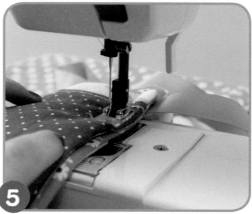

5 Machine-stitch along both sides of the pocket. You will be stitching through very thick layers. Take your time, turn the corners, include the ribbon ends in the seams, and close the opening in the stitching. Reinforce stitch when you get to the handles. If your machine can't sew through all the layers, you can hand-sew the sides together using a whipstitch.

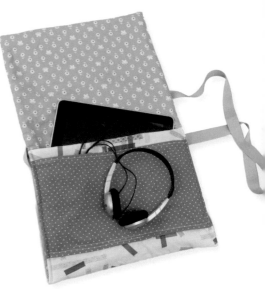

You are ready to pack your bag and hit the road!

I Made It Labels

Look at your clothes, accessories, even your stuffed animal. Labels are everywhere. They tell who made the shirt you are wearing. You make things too, so let everyone know by making your very own labels. What is your label? Is it your name or a fun saying?

What You Need

x Twill tape, at least ¾ inch-wide
x Fabric markers
x Scissors
x Fray Check* or craft glue

*Fray Check is special glue that is made just for stopping the fray on the ends of fabric. If you don't have Fray Check, you can use craft glue instead.

1 *Write with the fabric markers directly onto the twill tape. It's easy to make lots of tags at once and then keep them for when you make something new.*

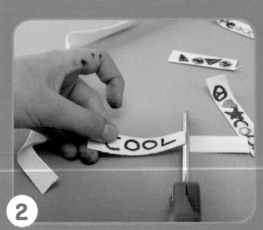

2 *Trim the twill tape, leaving an edge on both sides of your words or design.*

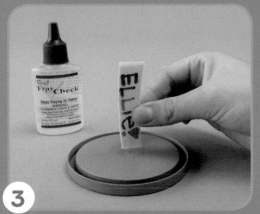

3 *So that the edges don't fray, dip them in a little Fray Check or craft glue. Then, put them on a piece of paper to dry.*

4 *When the tags are dry, you can sew them onto your projects using a reinforce stitch (page 34).*

5 *Now everyone will know that you made it yourself!*

99

TIME TO PLAY

It's time to step away from your sewing machine and cut loose. Do you like to plan parties? Or maybe you've always wanted to form your own band. Sometimes it's fun just to chill with friends. Work hard and play hard. Make that your motto!

☆ *easy*   ☆☆ *medium*   ☆☆☆ *hard*

Hip Hip Hooray! Bunting ☆

What You Need

- Pattern for Hip Hip Hooray! Bunting
- 9 fabric scraps, each as big as a sheet of paper
- 1 package of medium rickrack
- Chalk
- Scissors
- Straight pins
- Ruler
- Sewing machine and thread

Bunting makes every day special!

LET'S REVIEW

Adding trim (page 40)

A NOTE FOR GROWN-UPS

Bunting is a quick and fun project. Young sewers might need help positioning flags onto the rickrack.

MAKE IT YOURS

- *Change the size or even the shape of the flags.*
- *Add letters to your flags to spell a word.*
- *Use ribbon or bias tape instead of rickrack.*
- *Sew by hand.*

1 Find the Hip Hip Hooray! Bunting pattern in the back of the book and use chalk to trace it onto fabric nine times. You can use a different piece of fabric for each flag.

2 Cut out fabric pieces.

3 Lay out the nine flags in the order you want them.

4 When you have them just right, stack up the flags with the first one on top.

5 With chalk, mark 10 inches from the end of the rickrack.

6 Pin your first flag onto the rickrack, starting at the chalk mark. The rickrack is on top of the flag.

"I love making bunting. It's an obsession!"
— FRANCES, 9

7 Machine-stitch through the center of the rickrack to attach the flag. The rickrack should be on top of the flag. Keep your stack of flags nearby.

8 As you finish sewing on the first flag, put the next flag under the rickrack and keep sewing.

9 Keep adding flags until they are all sewn on.

10 Hang up your bunting and celebrate!

Hip Hip Hooray! Wee Bunting

Dress up your cake or a tiny tree with this wee little bunting. It's made the same way as the big bunting, only smaller.

What You Need

- x Felt scraps
- x Scissors
- x Sewing machine and thread
- x Bamboo skewers if you are making cake bunting

1 Cut out 10 little triangles from felt scraps. They should be about 1 inch wide across the base.

2 Stack the triangles in the order you want them. The first one should be on top.

TIP: To decorate a cake, tie each end of the bunting to a bamboo skewer and stick into your cake.

3 Machine-stitch the triangles together. Since they are so small, it can be tricky to get them through the machine. First, pull the bobbin and top thread to make a long thread tail at the beginning. For each triangle, lift up the presser foot and slide the edge of the triangle under. Put down the presser foot and sew across the triangle. Sew a little space between each triangle and repeat. When all the triangles are sewn together, leave a long tail of threads at the end of the bunting.

P.S. You can make your wee bunting in all sorts of shapes too!

Quiet Play ☆☆

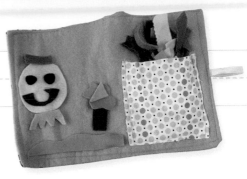

What You Need

- x Pattern for Perfect Pocket
- x 1 felt square
- x Cotton fabric as big as the felt square
- x Cotton fabric scrap for pocket
- x Felt scraps
- x 8 inches of ¾-inch-wide elastic
- x Chalk
- x Scissors
- x Straight pins
- x Ruler
- x Sewing machine and thread

Shhh...I'm busy creating. This felt mat will keep you happy no matter where you are. You can make felt pictures or play a game!

LET'S REVIEW

Turn a corner (page 35)

Reinforce stitch (page 34)

Turn the good side out (page 36)

Topstitch (page 39)

A NOTE FOR GROWN-UPS

This little activity mat easily rolls up and goes with you when your sewer needs something to do. Help might be needed adding the elastic and topstitching the mat at the end. Experienced sewers may want to sew on a more finished pocket that requires using an iron.

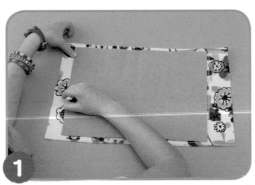

Use the felt square as your pattern and trace it with chalk onto your cotton fabric one time.

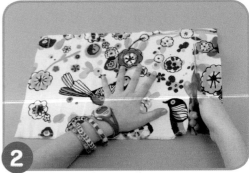

Cut out the cotton fabric.

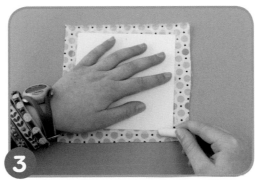

Find the Perfect Pocket pattern in the back of the book and use chalk to trace it onto cotton fabric one time. Cut out the pocket.

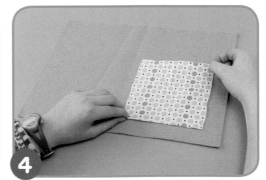

Place the pocket on the felt square about 1 inch from the right side and bottom edges. Pin it in place.

5 Beginning at the top right-hand corner, machine-stitch around three sides of the pocket; turn the corners. Leave the top unstitched.

The pocket will be on the inside.

6 Put the felt piece on top of the cotton fabric with the good sides together.

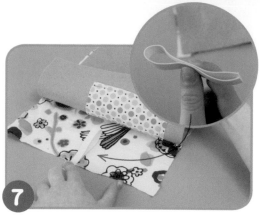

7 Fold the elastic piece in half and tuck the folded end between the fabric pieces on the same side as the pocket, about halfway down the side.

8 Pin the elastic in place. The loose ends of the elastic should stick out a bit.

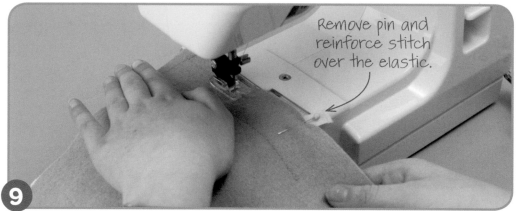

Remove pin and reinforce stitch over the elastic.

9 With chalk, mark start and stop sewing lines on one long side. Machine-stitch around the Quiet Play mat, starting at the start sewing marking. When you get to the elastic, remove the pin and reinforce stitch over the elastic.

10 Reach into the opening and turn the mat good side out. If it's really lumpy, ask an adult to help you iron the mat flat.

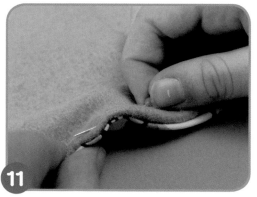

11 Fold in the seam allowances at the opening and pin them closed.

12 Topstitch around the entire Quiet Play mat. Be sure to stitch the opening closed and turn the corners.

13

Fill the pocket with felt scraps of different shapes and sizes. You might want to cut some into shapes you like.

When you are finished, you can easily roll and go!

Being quiet has never been so much fun!

MAKE IT YOURS

* *Review how to make a Perfect Pocket (page 58) to make a pocket with finished sides.*

* *You can make any kind of game you want. You just have to cut out the felt pieces you need.*

* *Decorate the outside before machine-stitching so everyone will know that it's yours.*

* *Make a double-sided pocket out of cotton fabric and attach it to the mat with ribbon.*

* *Change the size of the Quiet Play mat. It can be as big or as small as you want it to be.*

Tic-Tac-Toe Game

1. *Cut four strips of felt all the same length to form the Tic-Tac-Toe board.*
2. *With chalk, draw five X's and five O's onto felt scraps.*
3. *Cut around the chalk marks so you have felt X's and O's.*
4. *Lay down your felt strips and find someone to play with you.*

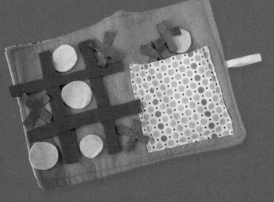

Tic-tac-toe, three in a row!

Etc. Backpack ☆☆

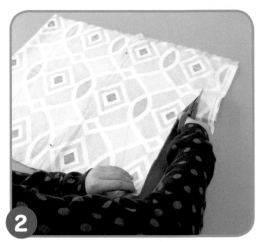

What You Need

- x Pattern for Etc. Backpack
- x ½ yard cotton fabric
- x 3½ yards of ½-inch-wide ribbon
- x Chalk
- x Scissors
- x Straight pins
- x Safety pin or bodkin
- x Iron and ironing board
- x Sewing machine and thread

LET'S REVIEW

Reinforce stitch (page 34)

Make a casing (page 114)

Iron safely (page 22)

A NOTE FOR GROWN-UPS

The construction of the bag is similar to the Water Bottle Holder (page 139). Your sewer might need help adding the tabs at the bottom of the bag and threading the ribbon through the casing and tabs. Also, an iron is needed for creating the casing.

This is the perfect bag to hold your stuff, no matter where you're going or what you're doing!

Place bottom of pattern along fold.

1 Fold your fabric in half so the good sides are together. Find the Etc. Backpack pattern in the back of the book. Place the bottom of the pattern along the fabric fold and use chalk to trace it onto fabric one time.

2 Place a few pins in the folded fabric so the layers don't shift. Cut out the fabric. Do not cut along the fold. After cutting, you will have one piece of fabric.

Make a casing on both short ends of the fabric, but don't put the ribbon in the casings yet. Just turn to page 114 for detailed directions on How to Make a Casing.

TURN THE PAGE →

"I'd use it for ballet or sports. I like basketball best."
— **FRANCES, 9**

MAKE IT YOURS

* *Change the size of the bag.*

* *Add a pocket on the outside of the bag.*

* *Use the pattern to make a simple tote with ribbon handles.*

* *Don't add the tabs and you have a large drawstring bag.*

Make a drawstring bag!

Add a pocket!

cut two pieces of ribbon, each 3 inches long.

3 Make casings as shown on page 114. Then fold the fabric in half with the good sides together so the casings match up. Pin the casings together.

4 Time to make the tabs. The tabs will guide the ribbon to make backpack straps. Cut two pieces of ribbon each 3 inches long.

5 Fold the ribbons in half and pin each one about 1½ inches up from the bottom fold on each side of the bag. The loose ends of the ribbons should stick out.

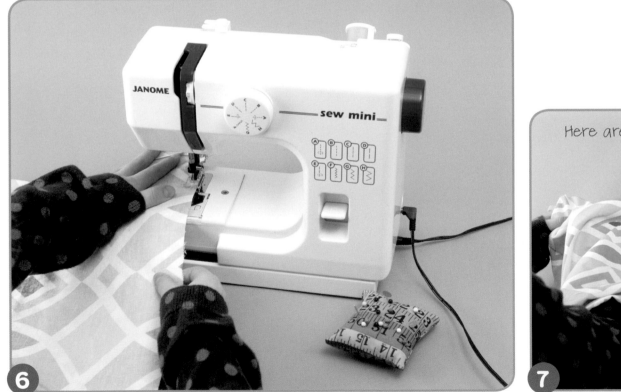

6 Machine-stitch the sides closed; begin stitching at the bottom edge of the casing. Be careful not to sew the casing closed. Reinforce stitch at the ribbon tabs.

Here are the little tabs.

7 Remove any pins. Turn the bag good side out.

8 Time to add the ribbon. Using a safety pin or bodkin, push and pull the ribbon through one of the casings.

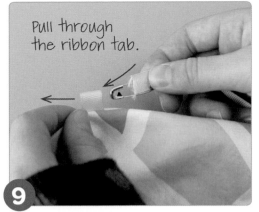

Pull through the ribbon tab.

9 Now, take the ribbon down along the same side of the backpack and through the ribbon tab and then back up.

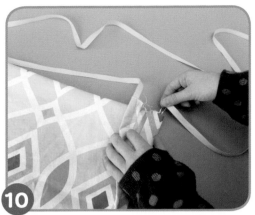

10 Push and pull the ribbon through the other casing.

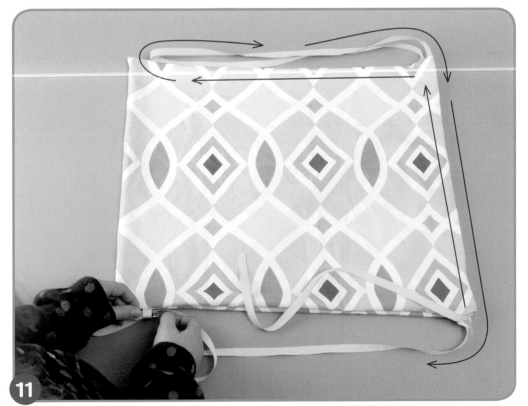

11 Take the ribbon down along the other side of the backpack and through the other tab and then back up to the top.

12 Tie the ends of the ribbon together in a tight knot. Be sure that the ribbon is lying flat.

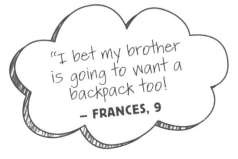

"I bet my brother is going to want a backpack too!
— FRANCES, 9

GO TO NEXT PAGE

13

Pull the ribbon straps to close the top of the bag and try it on. If the straps are too long for you, cut off enough of the ribbon so the backpack fits you comfortably and retie the ends.

Fill up your backpack, pull the ribbon straps to close the bag, and head out to have some fun!

How to Make a Casing

A casing is a narrow tube that you can thread ribbon or elastic through to make a drawstring bag or a skirt. It is made like a hem, but the second fold is a little wider so you can thread ribbon through it. Once you can make a simple casing, you can use it for many projects!

1

Lay out the fabric with the good side down. Fold the edge where you want the casing ½ inch to the wrong side so the good side is showing. Iron it flat.

2

Fold over the same edge 1 inch and iron.

3

Machine-stitch along the inner edge of the fold.

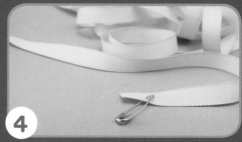

4

When it's time to put in the ribbon or elastic, attach one end of the ribbon or elastic to a safety pin or bodkin.

you made a casing!

5

Use your thumbs to push the safety pin and pull the ribbon or elastic through the casing until it comes out the other end.

Superstar Microphone ☆☆

What You Need

- x Pattern for Superstar Microphone Handle
- x Pattern for Superstar Microphone Top
- x 2 felt squares
- x Chalk
- x Scissors
- x Straight pins
- x Hand sewing needle and thread
- x Sewing machine and thread
- x Stuffing

yes, you are a singing superstar!

LET'S REVIEW

Turn a corner (page 35)

Hand-sew a running stitch or whipstitch (page 151)

Turn the good side out (page 36)

A NOTE FOR GROWN-UPS

A microphone is a must for any budding superstar! This one uses minimal machine sewing skills and can be easily made entirely by hand. Securing the top of the microphone to the handle can be a challenge for some.

1 Find the Superstar Microphone Handle pattern in the back of the book and use chalk to trace the pattern onto felt one time.

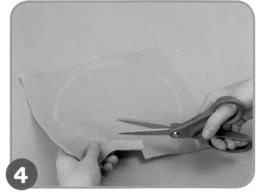

2 Cut out the handle.

3 Find the Superstar Microphone Top pattern in the back of the book and use chalk to trace the pattern onto felt one time.

4 Cut out the top piece.

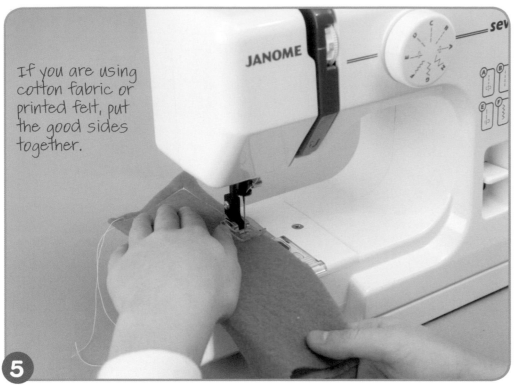

If you are using cotton fabric or printed felt, put the good sides together.

5 First, sew the handle. Fold the felt handle in half the long way. Beginning at the bottom corner at the fold, machine-stitch the short bottom edge, turn the corner, and stitch the long side edge. Leave the top open.

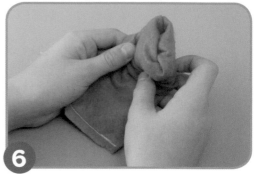

6 Clip the corners and turn the handle good side out.

7 Stuff the handle firmly. You want to make sure that it is stuffed well or your microphone will be floppy.

Do not knot the thread at the end of sewing.

8 Now sew the top of the microphone. Cut a long piece of hand sewing thread. Sew a running stitch around the edge of the top. Do not knot the thread at the end of sewing. If your thread gets short, just pull the thread so that the fabric bunches up and keep sewing.

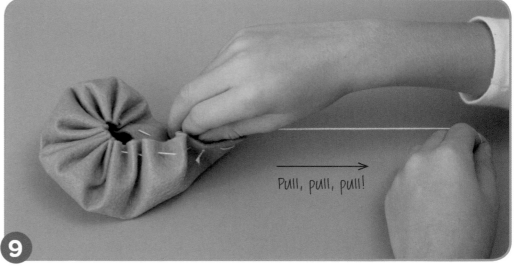

Pull, pull, pull!

9 Gently pull, pull, pull the thread until the top of the microphone forms into a ball. Don't cut the thread.

10 Carefully open up the ball and stuff it.

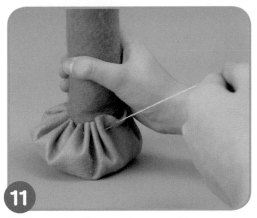

11 Let's put it all together now! Insert the open end of the microphone handle into the top of the microphone. Pull the thread on the microphone top to get a good fit. Once you have it the way you like it, knot off the thread close to the microphone.

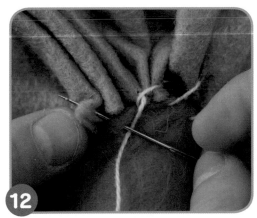

12 Hand-sew the microphone top to the handle, using a whipstitch. Push the needle through both the microphone top and handle to secure it. Sew all the way around the top and knot off.

Time to sing your heart out!

MAKE IT YOURS

* *Add on/off buttons to your microphone.*

* *A length of craft thread on the bottom can be a microphone cord.*

* *Make it with cotton fabric.*

* *Hand-sew the microphone.*

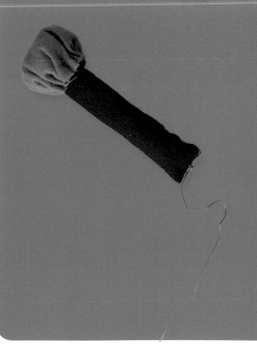

Rock On Guitar ☆☆☆

Imagine the crowd, the lights, the music, the guitar. Rock on!

LET'S REVIEW

Sew in a circle (page 136)

Hand-sew a running stitch or whipstitch (page 151)

A NOTE FOR GROWN-UPS

This project has multiple steps and may require a few sewing sessions to complete. Remind your child to leave two openings for stuffing. Help may be needed attaching the guitar strings.

1 Find the Rock On Guitar pattern in the back of the book. Use chalk to trace the pattern onto felt two times.

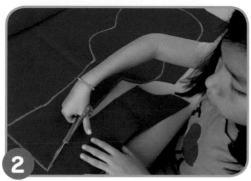

2 Cut out the felt guitars.

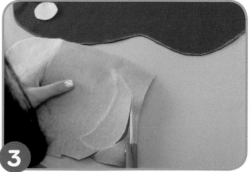

3 Time to customize your guitar. How will it look? What colors will you use? Use felt scraps to cut out shapes, letters, and designs to decorate your guitar.

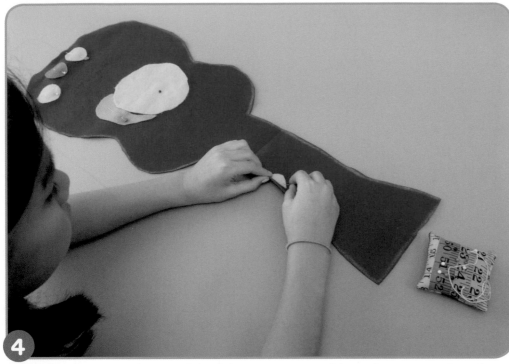

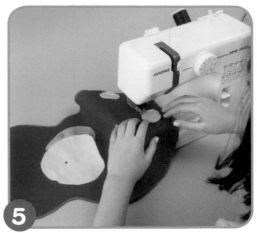

4 Place the shapes onto one of the felt guitar pieces. Move them around until you like the way they look, then pin them in place.

5 Machine-stitch the felt pieces onto the guitar. Take out the pins as you sew. After sewing on a section, remove the guitar from the machine and cut your threads then continue sewing another section. Take your time.

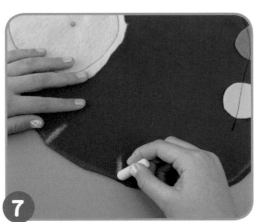

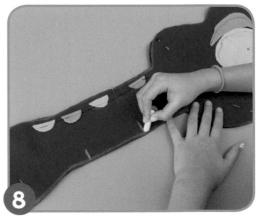

6 Put the top of the guitar onto the other guitar piece with the good sides facing out. Pin the pieces together around the edges.

7 Since the guitar is so big, you need to make two holes for stuffing. With chalk, mark start and stop sewing lines on the body of the guitar. Make the distance between the two lines about as long as your index finger.

8 Make a second set of start and stop sewing lines on the neck, or long part, of the guitar.

TURN THE PAGE

"It's so fun! It makes me feel crazy when I play it."

— ANNA MERCEDES, 10

Sewing Playlist

Here are some of our favorite songs for rocking out while you sew. Download them from the web and make your own mix tape!

▶ "Hey Boy" The Magic Kids

▶ "I'm Sticking with You" The Velvet Underground

▶ "Walking the Dog" Rufus Thomas

▶ "Motor Away" Guided by Voices

▶ "A Girl Like You" The Troggs

▶ "Hey Now" Talking Heads

▶ "Follow the Leader" Eric B. & Rakim

▶ "Bar-B-Q" Wendy Rene

▶ "Dedicated Follower of Fashion" The Kinks

▶ "Ham 'n' Eggs" A Tribe Called Quest

▶ "Thread the Needle" Clarence Carter

▶ "Enjoy Yourself" The Specials

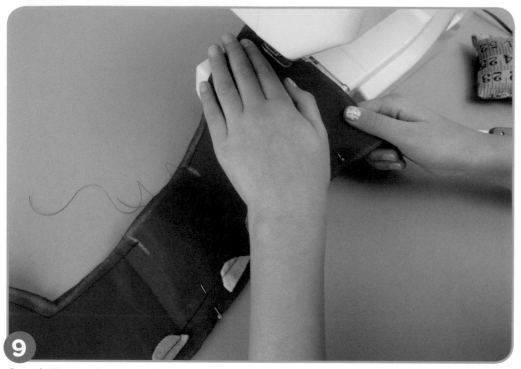

TIP: The shape of the guitar will curve, go straight, and turn corners. Guide your machine around the fabric, keeping the presser foot along the edge.

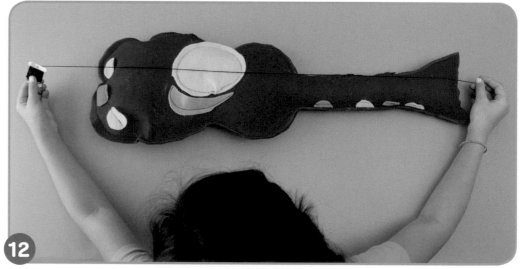

9

Carefully machine-stitch the guitar together. Begin at the start sewing line on the body of the guitar. Be sure to stop sewing and reverse stitch when you get to the first line on the neck of the guitar. Take the guitar off the machine and cut the threads. Then, begin sewing again (and reverse stitch) at the second marked line on the neck. Continue sewing all the way back around to the stop sewing line on the body and reverse stitch.

10

Once you are finished, stuff the guitar through both openings. You want to stuff the neck so that it is stiff and won't flop. The body of the guitar can be a little softer.

11

Hand-sew both openings closed with a whipstitch.

12

Your guitar needs some strings! Measure six lengths of craft thread; each should be a few inches longer than your guitar. Cut the six strings.

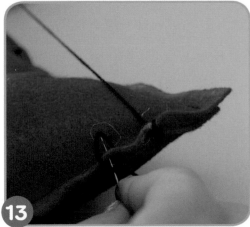

13 Hand-sew the six strings onto the guitar. For each thread, bring the thread up through the neck end of the guitar and loop the needle back around the edge to form a knot so that the string stays on.

14 Guide the thread down to the other end of the guitar and hand-sew the other end of the thread on, looping it around the edge before knotting off. Repeat for all six strings.

Time to rock 'n' roll!

MAKE IT YOURS

* *Change the size and shape of the guitar. Maybe you'll play a bass guitar or a Flying V.*

* *Use cotton fabric.*

* *Add a guitar strap using a yard of wide ribbon.*

* *Embellish the guitar with buttons and trims.*

* *Hand-sew the guitar.*

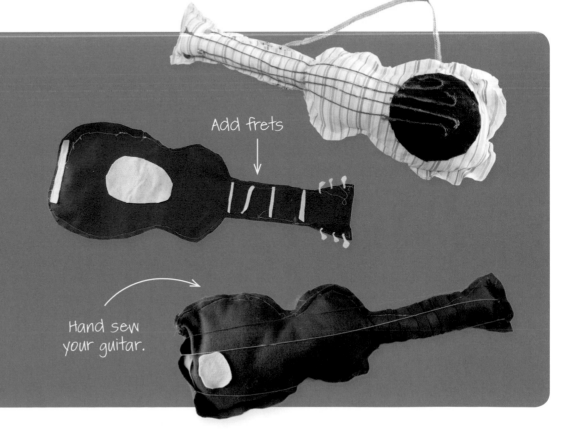

Add frets

Hand sew your guitar.

THE GREAT OUTDOORS

Planning your next adventure? Be prepared because you never know what to expect from Mother Nature. Make a Snack Time bag to hold your trail mix or a Portable Tree Stump to take a break and enjoy the view. Now get out there and explore!

☆ *easy*　　☆☆ *medium*　　☆☆☆ *hard*

Snack Time  ☆

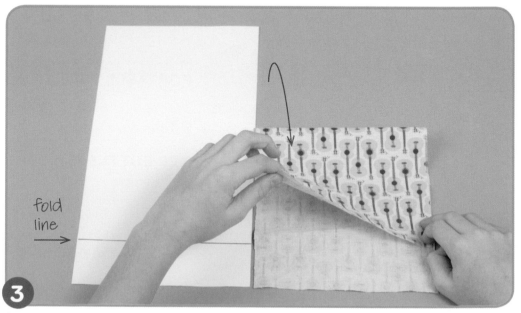

What You Need

- x Pattern for Snack Time
- x ¼ yard cotton fabric
- x 3½-inch-long piece of self-adhesive hook-and-loop tape
- x Chalk
- x Scissors
- x Straight pins
- x Sewing machine and thread

LET'S REVIEW

Turn a corner (page 35)

A NOTE FOR GROWN-UPS

This project is so quick to make, your young sewer will want to make several at a time to use for school snacks and outdoor adventures. Once the snack is gone, the bags can be machine-washed and filled again and again. New sewers may need help turning corners and attaching the hook-and-loop tape.

Don't use plastic bags when you're on the trail; use this handy reusable pouch instead! It's perfect for snack time, no matter where you are.

1 Find the Snack Time pattern in the back pocket of the book. Use chalk to trace the pattern onto the fabric one time. Cut out the fabric.

2 Machine-stitch straight across one short end of the fabric. This is called a staystitch and it is done through one layer of fabric so the edge doesn't fray. Trim the threads.

fold line →

3 Lay out the fabric with the good side down, the stitched edge at the top, and the pattern piece next to it. Fold the stitched edge of the fabric down to the fold line on the pattern. Pin the side edges together.

Trail Mix

Whether you hit the open trail or are just going across town, it's always nice to have a little snack. Here is Jackson's favorite recipe, but you can change up the ingredients and amounts to suit your taste.

- x 1 cup dry cereal
- x 2 cups pretzel sticks
- x ¼ cup chocolate chips
- x ¼ cup white chocolate chips
- x ¼ cup raisins

Mix it all up in a big bowl and scoop into your Snack Time bag. Store any extra Trail Mix in an airtight container.

Happy snacking!

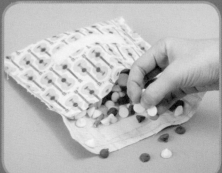

127

MAKE IT YOURS

* *Draw or stitch your own design or your name on the pouch.*

* *Change the size of the case to fit different snacks or other things like a camera or MP3 player.*

* *Use a button to close it.*

* *Line your Snack Time bag by using two pieces of fabric. Follow the steps in Turn the Good Side Out (page 36) and then jump to step 4.*

* *Sew the pouch by hand.*

4

Machine-stitch around the entire pouch. Start at a bottom corner. Go up, across the top, and down the other side.

TIP: you might sew with a zigzag stitch if the fabric frays a lot.

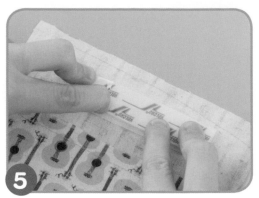

5

Time to add the hook-and-loop tape. Remove the paper backing from one side and stick that side of the hook-and-loop tape to the top flap.

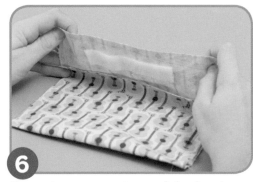

6

Keep the two sections of the hook-and-loop tape together and remove the other tape cover. Fold the top down so that the pouch opening is folded over a bit.

7

Press down hard so that the hook-and-loop tape will stick to both sides.

TIP: Iron the hook-and-loop tape so that it will stay in place better.

Open and fill with your favorite snack!

"The white chocolate chips make my trail mix extra yummy!"
— JACKSON, 11

Extra Pocket & Belt ☆

What You Need

- x Chalk
- x Scissors
- x Straight pins
- x Hand sewing thread and needle
- x Sewing machine and thread

POCKET:

- x Pattern for Extra Pocket
- x 1 felt square
- x Button

BELT:

- x 1½ yards of 1-inch-wide ribbon or webbing
- x 2 D-rings, 1 inch wide

LET'S REVIEW

Turn a corner (page 35)

Sew on a button (page 152)

Reinforce Stitch (page 34)

A NOTE FOR GROWN-UPS

This two-part project is popular with kids of all ages. When making the pocket, new sewers might need help cutting the slit and sewing on the button. Measuring around his or her own waist can also be tricky.

You can always use an extra pocket on your belt!

MAKE THE POCKET

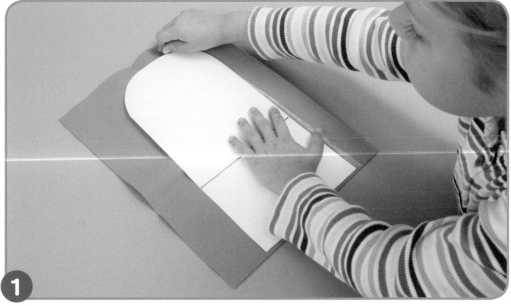

1 Find the Extra Pocket pattern in the back of the book and use chalk to trace it onto felt one time.

2 Cut out the felt piece.

3 Fold the felt in half so that the top and bottom match up.

TIP: you can mark the slits with chalk first.

4 Cut two slits along the fold about 1½ inches in from each side. The slits should be about ½ inch long.

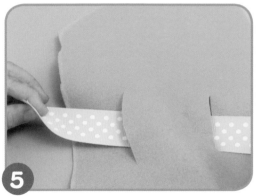

5 Check to make sure your belt ribbon fits through the slits. If it is too tight, cut the slits a little longer so the belt will fit.

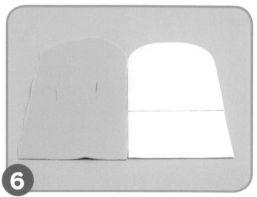

6 Open the felt piece and lay it next to the Extra Pocket pattern with the good side facing down.

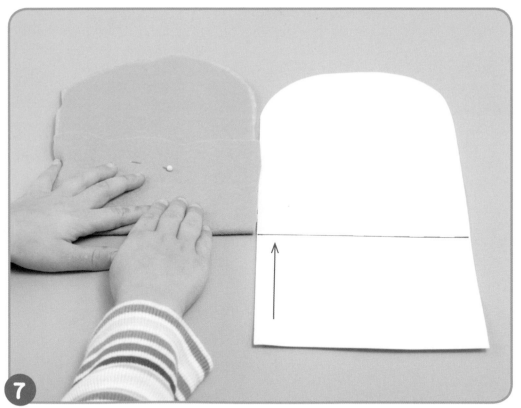

7 Fold the bottom of the pocket up so it lines up with the fold line on the pattern. Pin the fold in place.

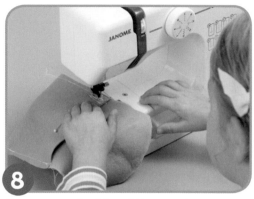

8 Sew up each side of the pocket.

9 Now it's time to add a button. Hand-sew the button to the center of the inside pocket 1½ inches from the top edge. Be careful not to sew the pocket closed! See page 152 for how to sew on a button.

TURN THE PAGE

"I like to walk around in leaves and collect different ones. Then I jump in the leaves!"
— **PHOEBE, 7**

MAKE IT YOURS

* *Make the pocket out of cotton fabric.*

* *Close it with hook-and-loop tape or a zipper.*

* *Just make the belt or the pocket.*

* *Decorate the pocket with your initials or a picture before sewing it.*

* *Sew by hand.*

* *Attach the pocket with hook and loop tape or a button.*

Add a zipper.

10

Make a buttonhole by folding the pocket flap down. Use chalk to mark the fabric where it covers the button. This is where you will make the buttonhole.

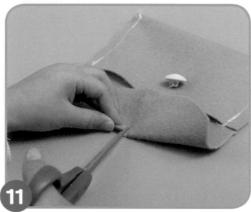

11

Fold the felt at the chalk mark. Cut a small slit at the marking to make the buttonhole.

TIP: If you use cotton fabric that frays, you will need to hand-whipstitch around the buttonhole opening.

Button up!

MAKE THE BELT

This simple D-ring belt goes great with your Extra Pocket or you can wear it alone.

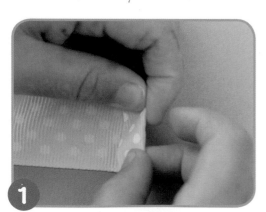

1

Fold one end of your ribbon or webbing under two times.

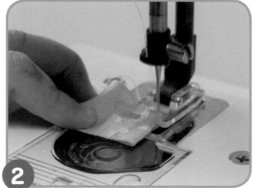

2

Machine-stitch along the fold. Reinforce stitch by sewing forward all the way across the fold, then reversing back the entire length of the fold.

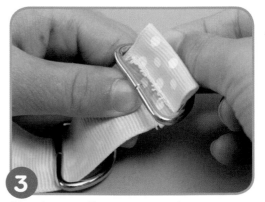

3

Slip the two D-rings onto the sewn edge.

4 Fold the belt over about 1½ inches and pin the edge in place.

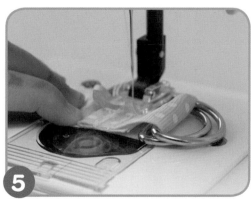

5 Machine-stitch the stitched edge down to the belt. Reinforce stitch by sewing all the way across and then reverse back the whole way so that the stitches will be strong.

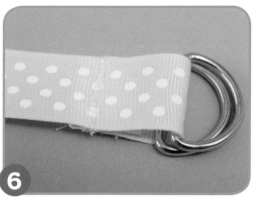

6 The D-rings are sewn onto the belt.

7 Try on the belt so that you get a good fit. Pull the belt so it feels good and cut it so that the tail is not too long.

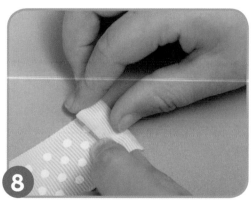

8 Fold the cut end of the belt over twice as in step 1.

9 Reinforce stitch by machine sewing all the way across it and reverse along the fold like you did in step 2.

> **To put your belt on, slide the end of the belt through both D-rings and then back through the first ring.**

To put the belt on the Extra Pocket, weave the end of the belt through the slits in the pocket.

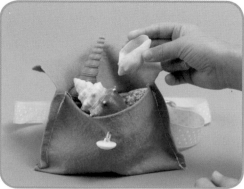

What will you put in your Extra Pocket?

"It's always nice to take a break when you're on a long hike."
— MADELINE, 9

Portable Tree Stump ☆☆

Sit down and enjoy the view. The outside pocket will hold your journal and guidebook.

What You Need

- x Pattern for Portable Tree Stump
- x ¾ yard cotton fabric for pillow
- x ½ yard cotton fabric for pocket
- x 1 yard of 1-inch-wide ribbon
- x Stuffing
- x Chalk
- x Scissors
- x Straight pins
- x Hand sewing thread and needle
- x Sewing machine and thread

LET'S REVIEW

Sew in a circle (page 136)

Turn the good side out (page 36)

Hand-sew a running stitch or whipstitch (page 151)

A NOTE FOR GROWN-UPS

What a clever way for kids to enjoy the great outdoors! This project requires a little more patience than others, but it is fun to make. Encourage your child to sew slowly around the circle shape. Adding the handle might require some help.

1 Fold the pillow fabric in half.

2 Find the Portable Tree Stump pattern in the back pocket. Use chalk to trace the pattern onto the folded fabric one time. Pin fabric layers together.

3 Cut out the fabric. You will have two circles.

GO TO NEXT PAGE

Sew in a Circle

Not all projects have corners. Sometimes you will sew around a circle or a curve like when you make a Cookie Coin Saver or Sleepy Bear. Practice sewing in a circle on your Stitching Sampler or by cutting out two medium-sized circles and sewing them together.

The trick to sewing in a circle is to go slow and keep your eye on the presser foot and the fabric. Never stop and raise the presser foot like when you turn a corner. Instead, slowly turn the fabric as you sew. Your hands will get closer together. Keep sewing until you are all the way around the curve. If you get off track, you can stop and readjust the presser foot onto the edge of the fabric, but be careful not to turn too sharply or your circle will be pointy!

Slide part of the pattern off the fabric.

4

To cut out a pocket, use the pattern for the Portable Tree Stump. ***Do not fold the pocket fabric.*** Place the pattern on top of the single layer of pocket fabric. Slide the top part of the pattern off of the fabric. Trace around the part of the pattern that is on the fabric.

5

Cut out the pocket. Place it on top of one of the pillow pieces matching the bottoms of the circles and with both good sides facing the same way. Pin them together.

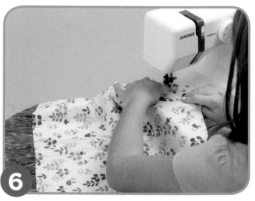

6

Leaving the top, straight part of the pocket open, machine-stitch around the curve of the pocket.

TIP: Are you worried about the top of your pocket fraying? If so, staystitch along the top, straight part of the pocket before pinning it to the circle. A zigzag stitch helps stop fraying too.

7

Lay the ribbon handle down in the middle of the pocket piece. Make sure it isn't twisted and position the ends of the ribbon so they stick out of the top a little bit.

8

Place the other fabric circle on top of the pocket and handle with the good sides together.

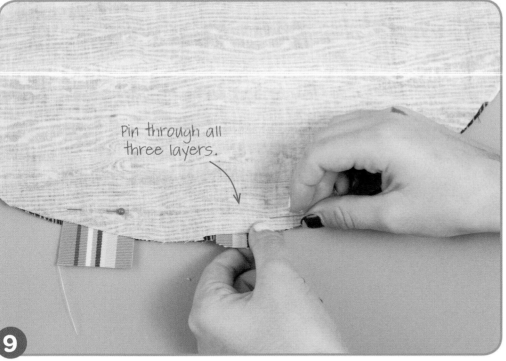

Pin through all three layers.

9

Get out your pincushion! Pin down the ends of the handle first, through all three layers. Then, pin all around the circle and even in the middle so that everything will stay put while you sew.

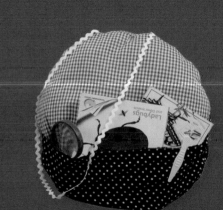

Change the pocket size, or make it without one.

GO TO NEXT PAGE

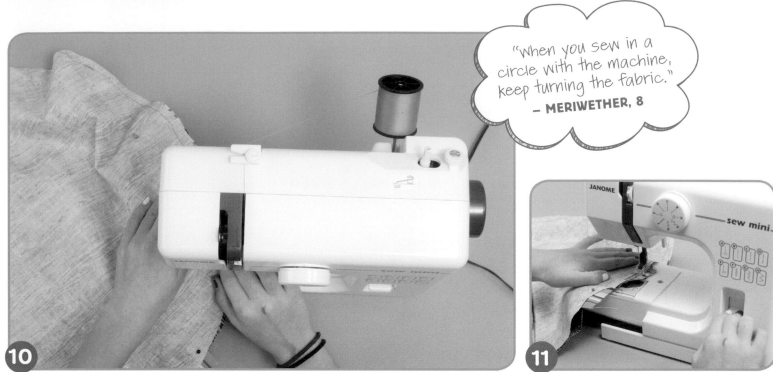

> "When you sew in a circle with the machine, keep turning the fabric."
> — MERIWETHER, 8

10

With chalk, mark start and stop sewing lines about 4 inches apart along the bottom of the circle. Machine-stitch around the edge. Take your time and gently turn the fabric as you sew. See how to sew a circle (page 136).

11

When you get to the handles, reinforce stitch by going across, reversing back, and then sewing across them again. This will make the stitches strong so that the handles won't pull out.

12

At the stop mark, reverse stitch and pull the fabric off the sewing machine. Remove any pins and turn the pillow good side out. Push around and smooth out the edges to form a circle.

13

Stuff the pillow so it is a little squishy, not too firm.

14

Fold in the seam allowances at the opening and hand-sew the pillow closed with a whipstitch.

Fill up the pocket with your journal and a good book and hit the trails!

Water Bottle Holder ☆☆

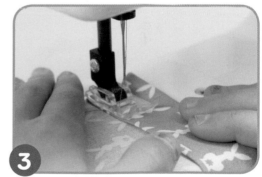

Keep hydrated and your hands free with this clever water bottle holder.

What You Need

- x Pattern for Water Bottle Holder
- x ¼ yard cotton fabric
- x 1 yard of 1-inch-wide ribbon or webbing
- x 18 inches of thin ribbon or yarn
- x Chalk
- x Scissors
- x Straight pins
- x Safety pin or bodkin
- x Sewing machine and thread

LET'S REVIEW

Turn a corner (page 35)

Reinforce stitch (page 34)

Make a casing (page 114)

Iron safely (page 22)

A NOTE FOR GROWN-UPS

Keeping cool and well hydrated has never been easier than with this hands-free water bottle holder. The construction of the holder is quite simple, but help might be needed making the casing and pulling the ribbon through. Also, sewing on the strap might take some patience.

1 Find the Water Bottle Holder pattern in the back of the book and use chalk to trace it onto fabric one time. Cut out of fabric.

2 Time to make a casing. Read the How to Make a Casing Skill Check on page 114 for detailed directions on how to make a casing. For this project, make a casing along each short edge. Fold and iron each short edge ½ inch to the wrong side. Then, fold and iron the short edges 1 inch more to the wrong side.

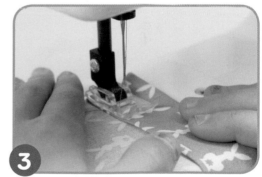

3 Machine-stitch the casings on both ends of the fabric. Position the fabric so that the edge of the presser foot runs along the inside of the fold. This way, you will have an opening for your ribbon. Carefully sew along the fold, reverse stitching at the beginning and ending of sewing.

GO TO NEXT PAGE

"I always carry a water bottle with me. You never know when you're going to get thirsty."
— ELLEN, 9

4 Fold the fabric with the good sides together and so the casings are matched up. Pin the layers together at the top.

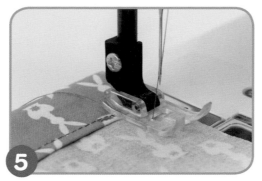

5 Machine-stitch the sides, starting just below the casing stitches. You do not want to sew all the way up to the top or you will not be able to thread your ribbon through the casing.

6 Turn the holder good side out.

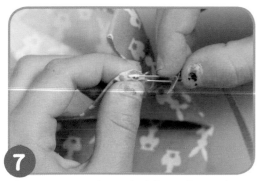

7 Now you can thread ribbon through the casing. Use a safety pin or bodkin to push and pull the ribbon through one casing.

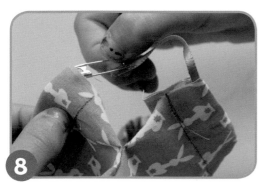

8 When you get to the end, continue going through the other casing. Keep pushing and pulling the ribbon through until it has gone through both sides.

Put a knot at the end.

Leave at least 6 inches

9 Once the ribbon is all the way through both casings, cut both ribbon ends so they are at least 6 inches from the bag and tie the ends of the ribbon together into a knot.

GO TO NEXT PAGE

MAKE IT YOURS

* *Change the size of the holder to fit your water bottle.*

* *Make each side with a different fabric.*

* *Just use it as a handy tote.*

* *Let everyone know it's yours by decorating the fabric before sewing the sides together.*

* *Sew by hand.*

10 Let's add the strap. Pin the ends of the strap on the opposite sides of the water bottle holder for balance. Pin each end of the strap ribbon under the casing about ½ inch from the side seam.

11 Open the water bottle holder and slide it onto the sewing machine so that only the top part will be sewn through.

12 Reinforce stitch the strap end to the water bottle holder by sewing forward and reverse several times so that it will stay on tight.

Fill your water bottle and hit the trail!

Patchwork Scarf ★★☆

Stay warm and toasty on your nature walk with this flannel-backed patchwork scarf.

LET'S REVIEW

Turn a corner (page 35)

Iron safely (page 22)

Turn the good side out (page 36)

Hand-sew a running stitch or whipstitch (page 151)

A NOTE FOR GROWN-UPS

Patchwork is fun and once young sewers nail down the basics, they can add patchwork details to almost any project. This project teaches sewers how to sew together squares. Since the project requires many steps, it might take your sewer several sessions to complete. Help might be needed sewing the backing fabric and patchwork fabrics together and turning the scarf good side out. Cutting and sewing the slit can also be tricky.

For a simpler version of the scarf, sew two long strips of fabric together and save the patchwork for another project. Making the slit to tie the scarf is optional as well.

SEW THE PATCHWORK

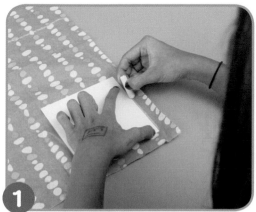

1 Find the pattern for the Patchwork Scarf Square in the back of the book and use chalk to trace it onto different fabrics 10 times. Use as many different fabrics as you want.

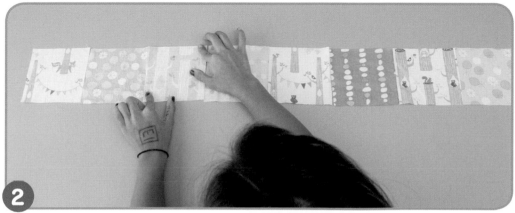

2 Cut out the fabric squares. Lay the squares in a line and decide how you want them to look when they are sewn into the scarf. Stack the squares up with the first one on top and the rest in the right order.

MAKE IT YOURS

* *Make both sides of the scarf in a solid fabric.*

* *Change the sizes of the patchwork squares.*

* *Add a button to keep the scarf closed.*

* *If your sewing machine makes buttonholes, make a buttonhole instead of a slit in the scarf.*

* *Or, don't make a slit and just tie the scarf around your neck.*

Put good sides together

3 Begin to sew the squares together. Take the top two squares off of the stack. Put the good sides of the fabric together.

4 Machine-stitch the squares together. Don't forget to reverse stitch at the beginning and end of each seam.

then add the next square

open the squares

5 Open the squares. Put the next square from the pile on the unstitched edge of the square with the good sides together. Machine-stitch them together.

TURN THE PAGE

"Will you make me a scarf too?"
– ROBBY THE DOG

145

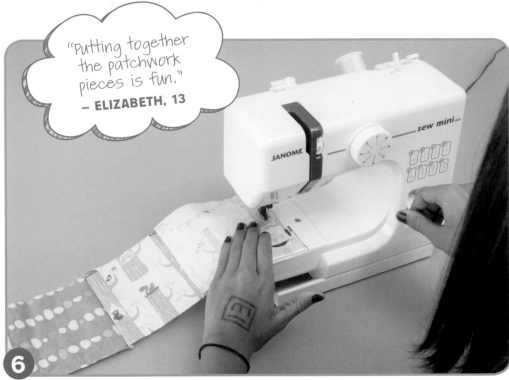

"Putting together the patchwork pieces is fun."
— ELIZABETH, 13

6 Keep adding squares and machine-stitching them until all 10 squares are sewn together.

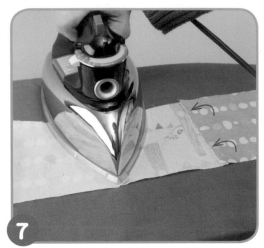

7 Have a grown-up help you iron the seam allowances down and over to one side.

ADD THE BACK

Put the end of the pattern along fold.

1 Now it's time to cut out the scarf fabric. Find the Patchwork Scarf pattern in the back of the book. Fold the flannel fabric in half with the good sides together and put the end of the pattern along the fold. Trace the pattern onto flannel fabric one time.

Do not cut the fold!

2 Pin the fabric layers together so they won't shift. Cut out the fabric. Be sure to cut through both layers of fabric and do not cut the fold.

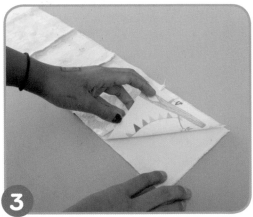

3 Unpin the fabric and open it up. Place the patchwork squares on top of the scarf piece with the good sides together.

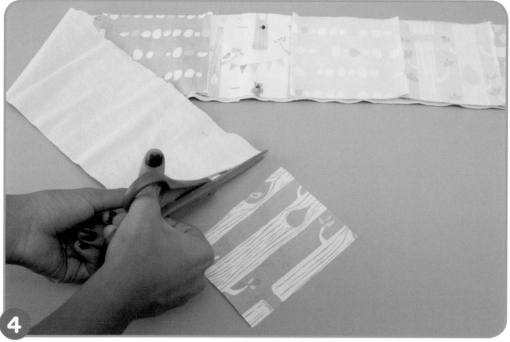

4 Pin the two layers together around all the edges. Trim off any extra patchwork that hangs off the end of the flannel scarf.

5 With chalk, mark start and stop sewing lines in the middle of one long side of the scarf. Make the marks about 5 inches apart. This will make it easier to turn the scarf good side out after sewing it.

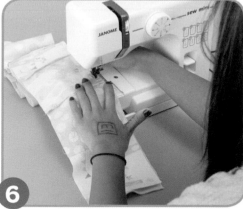

6 Machine-stitch all around the scarf, starting at the start sewing chalk line. Stop to take out pins along the way if needed. Stop sewing and reverse stitch at the stop sewing chalk line.

7 Clip the corner seam allowances near the stitches. Turn the scarf good side out. It's easy to pull one end of the scarf through the opening first and then the other end. Use a pencil or chopstick to gently push out the corners.

8 With adult help, iron the scarf flat and fold in the seam allowances at the opening. Pin the opening closed.

MAKE A SLIT

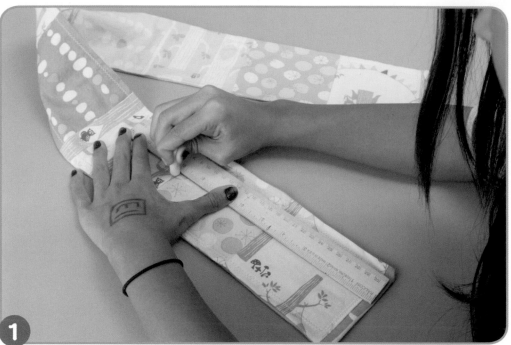

9

Set your sewing machine for a zigzag stitch. Topstitch all the way around the scarf making sure to stitch the opening closed.

1

Make a slit to tie the scarf. With chalk, measure 8 inches up from one end and mark a vertical line 2 inches long.

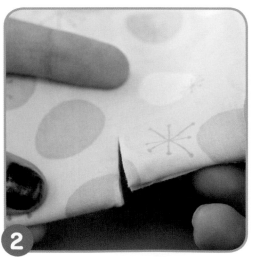

2

Fold the scarf in the middle of the chalk line and cut a slit along the line.

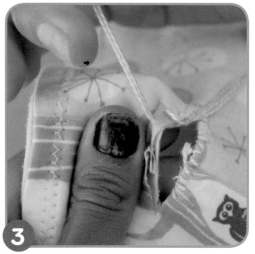

3

Using craft thread, sew a whipstitch around the edges of the slit. Make the stitches close together.

To tie your scarf around your neck, slide the end without the slit through the slit and gently pull it to tighten. Off you go on a nature hike! I wonder what you will discover.

Hand Sewing Skills

There are two hand sewing stitches that you will use to finish most of the projects in this book. Don't forget to knot your needle once you've threaded it, and to make another knot when you're done hand sewing.

How to Measure the Thread

We like to use the "Arm Length Rule" when cutting thread for hand sewing. To do this, cut a length of thread equal to the distance from your shoulder to your hand. No matter how young or old you are, if you follow this rule, you will always end up with the perfect length of thread.

ARM LENGTH RULE: from your shoulder to your hand = the perfect length!

How to Thread Your Needle

If you're sewing with craft thread:
Use a large-eye needle (we like the Chenille Size 22 Sharp Point Needle) and a LoRan Needle Threader.

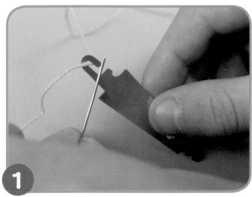

1 Push the hook or loop of the threader through the eye of the needle. Next, hook the thread.

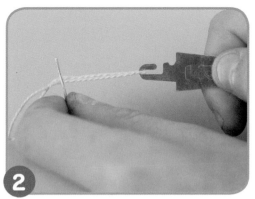

2 Pull the needle off the threader.

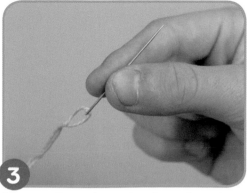

3 Keep pulling along the thread until the needle slides along one strand of thread. The needle is threaded!

If you're sewing with regular sewing thread:
Use a smaller needle and a wire needle threader.

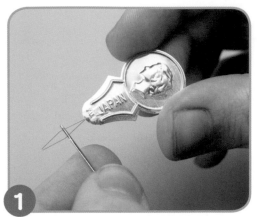

1 Put the loop of the threader through the eye of the needle.

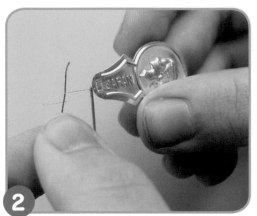

2 Stick your thread through the thin wire loop.

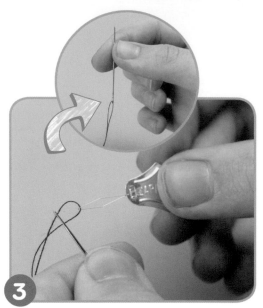

3 Pull the needle off the threader. Work gently, as the wire needle threader breaks easily. Keep pulling along the thread. The needle is threaded.

How to Tie a Knot

Once your needle is threaded, you need to knot the end of the thread to keep it from pulling through the fabric when you sew.

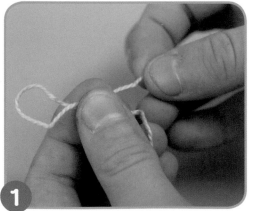

1 Make a loop at the end of the thread. If you're new to hand sewing, try winding the end of the thread around your finger. Slip the thread off your finger, and you've made a loop.

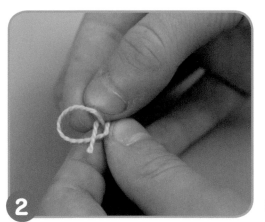

2 Bring the short end of the thread up through the loop.

"You can't make everything with a machine. You have to hand-sew, too."
— PATRICK, 11

3 Pull tight. You made a knot! Use these same steps to make another knot when you are finished sewing.

How to Sew a Running Stitch

The running stitch is like the straight stitch that you already know how to make on the sewing machine. When it's done right, the running stitch looks just like a dotted line.

TIP: Pinch the needle at the eye when you pull each stitch through. This way, the thread will not come out of the needle.

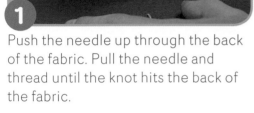

1 Push the needle up through the back of the fabric. Pull the needle and thread until the knot hits the back of the fabric.

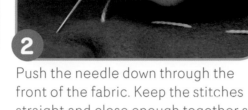

2 Push the needle down through the front of the fabric. Keep the stitches straight and close enough together so you don't have a big gap.

3 Bring the needle back up. Leave a little space between the needle and the last stitch. Repeat until you are finished!

How to Sew a Whipstitch

Use the whipstitch when you need to close the opening left between start and stop sewing marks. Or whipstitch a single fabric edge to decorate it and help keep the material from fraying.

1 Push the needle up through the back of the fabric. Pull the needle and thread until the knot hits the back of the fabric.

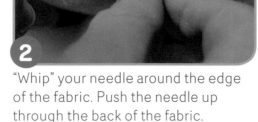

2 "Whip" your needle around the edge of the fabric. Push the needle up through the back of the fabric.

3 Make even stitches, only sewing up through the back of the fabric. Repeat until you are finished!

How to Sew on a Button

Are you sewing on a flat button or a shank button? Flat buttons have two or four holes for you to stitch through. Shank buttons have a little metal or plastic loop on the back. Either way, sewing on buttons is easy when you know the basic steps.

TO SEW A SHANK BUTTON:

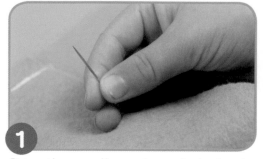

1 Bring the needle up through the back of the fabric.

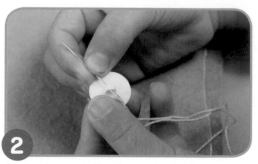

2 Slide the needle through the loop on the back of the button and push the button down to the fabric.

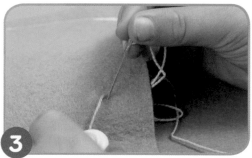

3 Sew back down through the fabric. Put the needle right back down into the fabric close to where you came up.

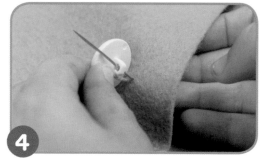

4 Now, sew back through the button loop and the fabric two or three more times so the button will stay put.

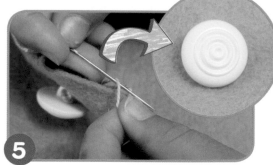

5 To finish, bring your needle to the back of the fabric and tie a knot.

TO SEW A FLAT BUTTON:

1 Bring the needle up through the back of the fabric.

2 Slide the needle through one of the holes in the button and push the button down to the fabric.

TIP: You can sew your stitches straight or make an x.

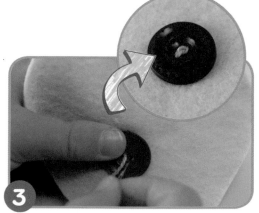

3 Sew back down through the fabric through another buttonhole. Keep sewing through all of the buttonholes at least two times. To finish, bring your needle to the back of the fabric and tie a knot.

Oops!

Fixing a mistake made on a sewing machine is a little harder than undoing your hand sewing stitches, but it can be done. When you see a problem, stop, and take your foot off the pedal. Take a deep breath, and think about how you might fix it. Here are some of the things that might happen when you're using a sewing machine and the ways to fix them.

How to Use a Seam Ripper

A seam ripper is a very sharp yet useful tool that can undo tiny machine stitches. Always store it in a safe place. When you need to use your seam ripper, take your time. Find a very bright light, or a sunny window, and sit nearby. Make sure the light is bright enough that you can see the stitches.

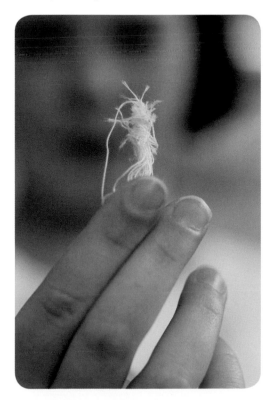

1 Gently separate the two fabric pieces with one hand. Hold the seam ripper in your other hand. At the end of the seam, carefully spear the first stitches with the seam ripper.

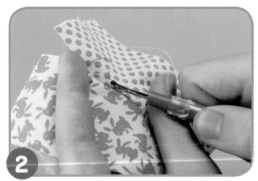

2 The sharp edge in the "u" of the tool will cut through your thread. Work slowly, being careful to cut your stitches, not the fabric.

3 Your stitches are coming undone!

Note: If you used the reverse stitch to make a knot, you may need to start an inch or so into the seam, then work backward.

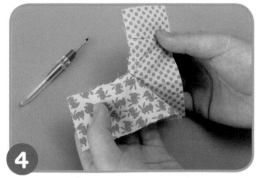

4 Lay down the seam ripper, and gently pull apart the two pieces of fabric. Continue these steps until your seam is completely undone.

How to Fix Common Problems

My seam is running off the edge of the fabric. You're not sewing in a straight line. Leave the old stitches where they are, lift the presser foot, and gently reposition the fabric to the place where you went off course. Carefully lower the presser foot so that you have a proper seam allowance of ¼ inch. Resume sewing.

Two pieces of fabric did not get sewn together. Either your fabric pieces aren't the same size, or you veered off the edge of your fabric. If you need to, trim the fabric so that both pieces are the same size. Leave the old stitches where they are. Go back to the beginning, and carefully lower the presser foot so that you have a proper seam allowance.

My thread keeps breaking. Your sewing machine might not be threaded correctly, the tension could be set wrong, or your needle might not be installed properly. Cut the old thread and discard. Rethread your sewing machine. Please refer to your sewing machine manual if this problem continues.

My thread keeps bunching up on the back of the seam. This happens when the bobbin thread and the needle thread aren't working together properly. First, double-check to make sure that you sewed with the presser foot in the "down" position. If not, drop the presser foot and resew. If you had the presser foot down and were sewing properly, rethread your sewing machine and take the bobbin out and put it back in.

Every time I finish sewing the needle comes unthreaded. You are cutting the thread too close to the needle. Remember the table rule (page 30). Once you finish sewing, lift the needle and the presser foot, and gently pull the fabric off the sewing machine. Now, as gently as you can, pull the threads down to the tabletop. Clip them close to the fabric instead of close to the machine.

My fabric got bunched up. This happens when you're not keeping your fabric flat as you guide it through the machine, especially when you're sewing large pieces of fabric. Be sure to smooth your fabric to make sure it's not folded or bunched as it travels past the needle. Once your fabric is bunched and stitched, the only way to fix it is to use a seam ripper to undo your stitches, and then start again.

My project is coming apart! Did you remember to reverse stitch when you started and stopped sewing? If not, your stitches will come undone.

The stitches aren't the same length. Remember how gently you need to hold the fabric while you guide it through the sewing machine? If your stitches are uneven, you are pulling too hard.

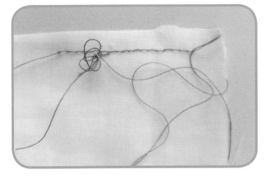

My needle broke. Double-check to make sure that you are using the right needle for your make and model of sewing machine. Did you accidentally sew over something you shouldn't have, like a pin or a metal zipper pull? Ask a grown-up to help replace the needle.

My needle broke!

My fabric is stuck in the machine. First, turn off and unplug your sewing machine. Lift the presser foot, and then use your right hand to manually turn the hand wheel toward you until the needle is in the up position. Now reach under the fabric to remove the

needle plate. You might have to take the bobbin out of its casing and then use the seam ripper or scissors to cut the tangle of threads that are clogging the feed dogs. Once you cut away the snarl, you can slowly ease your fabric away from the sewing machine.

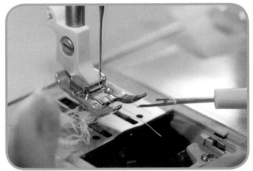

The good sides aren't facing out. Read the project directions to see how to put together the fabric when you sew. Did you put the good sides together first? The only way to solve this problem is to use a seam ripper to undo your stitches, reposition the fabric so the good sides are facing the right way, and resew your project.

"When you make a mistake, take a break. Once your brain has calmed down, you can fix what went wrong. Then keep on sewing!"
— MARY CLAIRE, 8

Sewing with a Group

When we decided to expand our initial Sewing School summer camp by offering lessons on sewing machines, we were a bit nervous. Just as teaching hand sewing had initially seemed quite daunting, we quickly came up with a simple system for teaching our young students how to sew on a machine.

We started small, with just a handful of kids who brought their own sewing machines. Their machines came from all over; some belonged to grandmothers, aunts, or parents, while others were still in their original boxes!

We gathered the children around and introduced them to the various parts of a sewing machine. We demonstrated how to thread the machine; we discussed bobbins, seams, and seam allowances. Then we moved onto a simple project, a square pillow that, with the input of our young sewers, ultimately evolved into the Secret Message Pillow (see page 54).

While machine sewing with a group of kids is very similar to hand sewing, the machines definitely add a twist! If you're teaching a large group, we recommend that you have a helper.

Instructional Tips

* Work with white thread, and pre-make several bobbins for quick change-outs. Place scissors and pincushions near each sewing machine.

* If you are providing the machines, label each with a number and create a sign-up sheet if you have more kids than machines. Remind young sewers that if they're waiting for an open machine, they can work on getting their project ready.

* Have a few hand sewing projects available.

* Don't let brand-new sewers work independently until they've had time to sew with you.

* Offer daily "teaching moments," using web videos and introducing projects with corresponding skills.

* When sewers ask for help, encourage them to problem solve. If something goes wrong with a machine, they can't just leave it!

* Be safe. Don't hand out seam rippers. Instead, require sewers to sign them out as needed and return them once they're done. Monitor the use of the iron unless you have permission from the parents and have watched the students use it.

For additional tips for group sewing, refer to our first book, *Sewing School*, or read our blog, *http://sewingschool. blogspot.com*.

Resource Guide

While you can find many sewing supplies around the house, you will have to purchase certain tools at specialty stores. An adult can help you locate the stores and the supplies that are just right for you.

Tools and Supplies

All of the materials and tools needed for your sewing kit as well as the other products we suggest, such as hook-and-loop tape and Fray Check, are available at most fabric and craft stores.

The Janome Sew Mini Sewing Machine, a kid-sized sewing machine we use with young sewers, is available at Hancock Fabrics (www.hancockfabrics.com), Home Depot, and many online stores.

Cotton Fabrics

A variety of printed and patterned cotton fabrics is available in retail stores nationwide. There are also many online sources that sell fabric. Following are a few of our favorites:

Fabricworm
www.fabricworm.com

ilovefabric
www.ilovefabric.com

Sew, Mama, Sew!
www.sewmamasew.com

superbuzzy
www.superbuzzy.com

Special Fabrics

Giant Dwarf
www.etsy.com/shop/giantdwarf
Felt

Modern June
www.etsy.com/shop/modernjune
Chalkboard fabric and oilcloth

Blogs and eMags for Kids Who Love to Sew

While the following websites are written for adults, they offer projects, tutorials, ideas, and resources for crafty kids.

Abby Glassenberg Design
www.whileshenaps.com

Bird and Little Bird
http://birdandlittlebird.typepad.com

BloesemKids
http://bkids.typepad.com

The Crafty Crow
www.thecraftycrow.net

Curly Birds
http://curlybirds.typepad.com

Kleas
http://kleas.typepad.com

maya*made
http://mayamade.blogspot.com

SouleMama
http://soulemama.typepad.com

Blogs That Inspire Us

As we craft with kids and in our everyday life, we find the blogs listed below to be sources of inspiration. These bloggers beautifully weave sewing in with their daily lives and busy families. While their featured projects are not specific to kids' sewing, many of the ideas could be adapted or sewn by an advanced young sewer with adult support.

The Long Thread
www.thelongthread.com

Posie Gets Cozy
http://rosylittlethings.typepad.com

Purl Soho
www.purlsoho.com

Sew Liberated
http://sewliberated.typepad.com

Wee Wonderfuls
www.weewonderfuls.com

Don't forget to check out the Sewing School blog! *http://sewingschool.blogspot.com*

INDEX

Page numbers in *italics* indicate photos or illustrations.

by Amie Petronis Plumley & Andria Lisle

Kids can complete these 21 inspired hand-sewing projects with minimal supervision. Step-by-step photographed instructions teach basic sewing skills, then put them to use making pillows, dolls, blankets, totes, and more.

Stitch Together Your Creativity Library with More Books from Storey

by Nicole Blum & Debra Immergut

You'll love sewing these playful one-of-a-kind accessories and imaginative home decor items. Easy instructions mean you can create any of the 101 beautiful and freestyle projects in less than a day.

by Nicole Blum & Catherine Newman

Create, hack, or customize! Step-by-step directions show you the basics of how to sew, embroider, knit, crochet, weave, and felt. You can then use your new skills to hand-make bracelets, backpacks, merit badges, keychains, and other stylish and practical items.

by Crispina ffrench

Re-purpose wool sweaters to create cool clothes, one-of-a-kind toys, and handy household items. Diagrams and detailed directions guide you through making zippered cardigans, rag dolls, potholders, and so much more!

Join the conversation. Share your experience with this book, learn more about Storey Publishing's authors, and read original essays and book excerpts at storey.com. Look for our books wherever quality books are sold or call 800-441-5700.